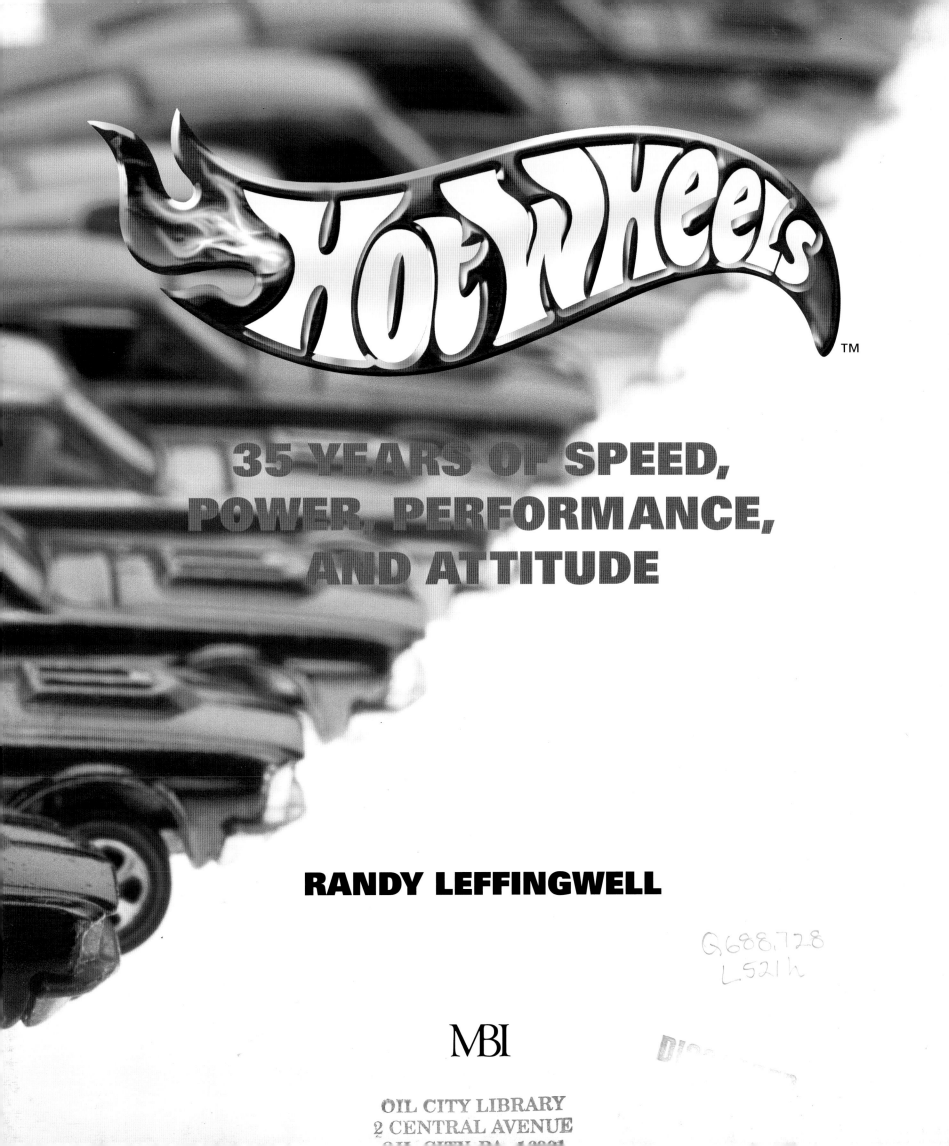

Hot Wheels™

35 YEARS OF SPEED, POWER, PERFORMANCE, AND ATTITUDE

RANDY LEFFINGWELL

MBI

This edition first published in 2003 by Motorbooks International, an imprint of MBI Publishing Company, Galtier Plaza, Suite 200, 380 Jackson Street, St. Paul, MN 55101-3885 USA

Motorbooks International titles are also available at discounts in bulk quantity for industrial or sales-promotional use. For details write to Special Sales Manager at Motorbooks International Wholesalers & Distributors, Galtier Plaza, Suite 200, 380 Jackson Street, St. Paul, MN 55101-3885 USA.

Library of Congress Cataloging-in-Publication Data

Leffingwell, Randy, 1948-
    Hot Wheels : 35 years of speed, power, performance, and attitude /
    Randy Leffingwell.
        p. cm.
    Includes index.
    ISBN 0-7603-1573-6 (hc : alk. paper)
    1. Hot Wheels toys—History. I.Title.

    TL237.2.L44 2003
    629.22'1—dc21

On the front cover: A rainbow of Hot Wheels cars.

On the title page: A spectraflame rainbow of Custom Mustangs.

On the back cover, top: Custom T-Bird. **Bottom:** Overbored 454.

Edited by Josh Leventhal and Amy Glaser
Designed by Koechel-Peterson

Printed in China

To Elliot Handler, for his clear vision of what children want to play with,

and for his dedication to push the idea of Hot Wheels cars through production

and into the hands of millions of children of all ages around the world.

And to my friend, Bruce Pascal, who opened my mind to the fascinating history

of Hot Wheels cars and Mattel that he encouraged me to write. Without Bruce's

own enormous research into this story, and without his generous willingness

to open dozens of doors for me, this book would not exist.

CONTENTS

Who would have known thirty-five years ago that a small piece of brightly colored die-cast metal with Redline wheels would affect so many lives?

Mattel grew steadily beginning in the 1940s under Ruth and Elliot Handler. The Barbie sensation of the 1950s took them even farther. With the introduction of Hot Wheels cars a decade later, Mattel grew to become the largest toy company in the world. Indeed, the Hot Wheels division itself could be considered the fifth-largest toy company today.

The vision of one man, Elliot Handler, has influenced many people. Through the years, children have played with these little toys called Hot Wheels cars. Many of these children grow up to become die-hard auto enthusiasts, attending races and car shows and working on their own vehicles. For some enthusiasts, the passion for owning these Hot Wheels cars becomes even stronger. They are the Hot Wheels collectors who relentlessly search for that special car missing from their personal collections.

In my case, from the first time I saw my friend's kids playing with that orange track and the Evil Weevil Hot Wheels car, I was hooked. When the offer came to design these cool cars, I figured I would try it for a few years until I could find a "real" job. Well, here I am thirty-four years later, and I still get a kick out of going to work and designing Hot Wheels cars with other crazy and creative people.

For the first twenty years there was only a handful of Hot Wheels employees. When I started in 1969, Elliot himself would sit in on our design meetings with our sketches—now called B sheets—pinned on the wall for review. Today this division in California consists of more than 200 people, with specialized areas such as computer graphics, licensing, automotive design, track and play sets, and new concepts. In addition, whole departments are devoted to promotions, packaging, marketing, the model shop, engineering, legal, and public relations, all working closely to produce these exciting toys. In fact, this is just a small part of the Hot Wheels worldwide family. In many countries, manufacturing, tooling, sales, and distribution are combined to meet the weekly demand for six million Hot Wheels cars.

I am often asked, "How can you keep coming up with new designs year after year?" That's the fun part! Wait until you see the next thirty-five years of Hot Wheels!

Larry F. Wood.

Memory can be a sometimes-fallible resource. The events, actions, thoughts, and decisions recorded here were important at the moment they occurred because they related to the work at hand: producing Hot Wheels cars. For most of the people who were involved in these situations, they and their activities were part of an ordinary workday in a volatile industry known as the children's toy business. As many of them said, no one expected Hot Wheels cars would become a subject for the study of history. Even Mattel, Inc. recognized the transitory nature of its occupation and let big chunks of its history go to collectors and to trash pick-up services. In addition, several key individuals are no longer with us for me to tap their memories, such as Ruth Handler and Jack Ryan. Several other people, for their own reasons, declined to speak with me for this book.

As a result of these challenges, there are bound to be errors in this book. I apologize for them in advance. As it is with all "histories" of ongoing phenomena, this Hot Wheels story will remain a work in progress. As you read, if something comes to you, some recollection, memory, or volume of written production records that will shed further light on this wonderful story and rectify any inaccuracies, I would like to hear from you. In the meantime, I hope you enjoy what several dozen deeply involved individuals recall about how it was then and is now.

I must thank Elliot Handler for creating these wonderful little cars, and for the time he spent with me recalling his part in their birth and early, formative years.

Within Mattel, Inc., today, I wish to acknowledge the help and encouragement of Amy Boylan, senior vice-president, New Media; John Handy, senior vice-president of design, Boys Division; Arun Kochar, director of manufacturing, Mattel, Inc., Penang, Malaysia; Heather Schneider, associate brand manager, Mattel Brands Consumer Products; Vicki Jaeger, brand manager, Mattel Brands Consumer Products; and Jim Wagner, senior vice-president of marketing, Boys Division.

I cannot express enough gratitude to Larry "Elwood" Wood, chief Hot Wheels designer, who took this project on as if it were his own, and provided regular infusions of history and hilarity. Larry was the first of the geniuses I met while doing this book, and he remains the most enjoyable of them all.

In addition to Larry, I am grateful to Carson Lev, director of Hot Wheels Adult Licensing, New Business Development as well as numerous Hot Wheels designers, engineers, and model makers who shared their time and enthusiasm.

Early on during the research for this book, I learned that many of Mattel's early employees call themselves members of the Mattel Alumni Association. That is because they credit "Mattel University" with an education far beyond—and much more fun than—any they received in formal institutions of learning. Among the Mattel Alumni, I am deeply indebted to Fred Adickes, Al Baginsky, Gene Barker, Dennis Bosley, Harry Bentley Bradley, Richard Caslow, Richard Chang, Bob Cowell, Marlene Dantzer, Sam Djujic, Pete Folger, Jerry Fyre, Derek Gable, Ira Gilford, Chuck Gode, Keith Johnson, Dave Keller, John Kensey, Alex Laird, Bernie Loomis, Jack Malek, Len Mayem, Lou Miraula, Luis Montes de Oca, Lenny Moquin, Steve Nelson, Howard Newman, Ralph Parris, Marshall Pearlman, Steve Pennington, Rita Rao, Carol Robinson, Bob Rosas, Walt Ross, Bill Rowley, Floyd Schlau, Frank Sesto, George Soulakis, Bill Summerfield, Joe Whitaker, Hiroe Okubo Wolf, and Charlie Wyle.

Outside the Alumni Association, but no less valuable in their contributions to making the cars great, successful, fast, and legendary, were Stan Christensen, Tom "the Mongoose" McEwen, Michael Otte, Arthur Russell, the late Ken Sanger, and Victor Savikas. I also thank Charles Kitson for his insight into collectors throughout the world.

For the cars, accessories, track, and incredible memorabilia photographed and shown in this book, I am grateful to Luis Montes de Oca, Gary Nabors, Bruce Pascal, Curtis Paul, Casey Barr, Bob Rosas, George Soulakis, and Larry Wood.

To my son Paul and my good friend Casey Barr, I owe thanks for keeping me focused on the fun of the cars. Further thanks goes to Casey for helping me develop the scale-model "studio" I used to photograph the cars.

To my two editors at MBI Publishing, Amy Glaser and Josh Leventhal, I owe thanks for their patience and direction. To my friend and former editor at MBI, Zack Miller, vice-president of publisher, I owe deep thanks for trusting me with this project.

Finally, to my love, Carolyn, thank you for your faith in me.

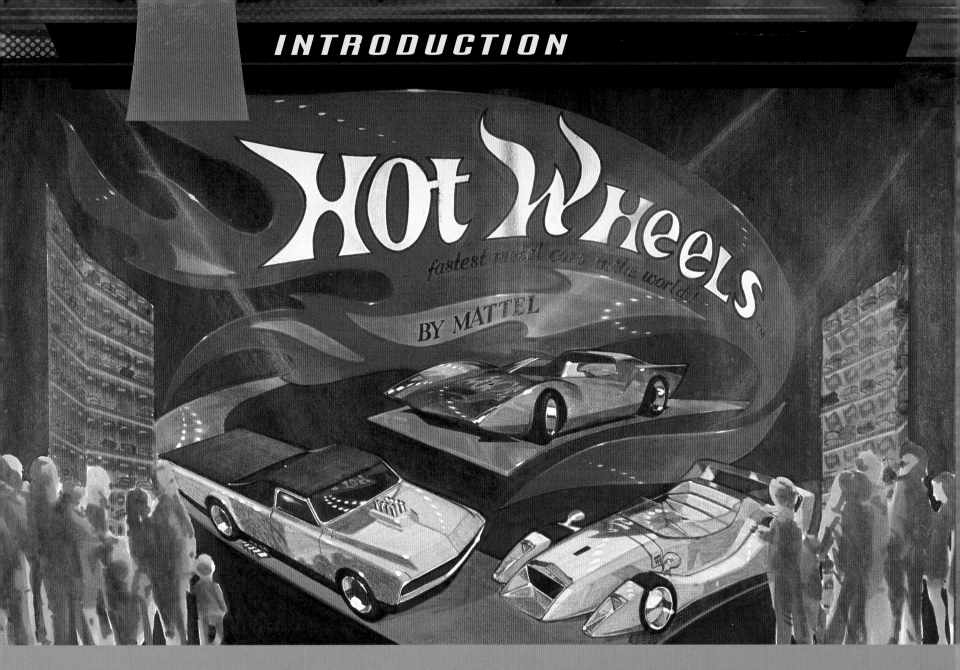

In the course of their thirty-five-year history, Hot Wheels cars have come to represent the ultimate in die-cast toy cars. This rich history is being told in its completeness here for the first time. One sense of perspective necessary to even understand why Hot Wheels cars deserve this consideration is to remember that these vehicles are toys from Mattel. To Mattel founders Elliot and Ruth Handler and their friend Harold Matson, the driving force was that any toy they created had to have the down-to-earth necessity of "play value." Mattel toys, especially Hot Wheels cars, were never intended to be displayed on a shelf if a child instead could sit down on the floor and create his or her own fantasy world with the car or doll. Mattel offered them the tools, of course, to build highways with banked turns and loop-the-loop daredevil tricks or to fit mature girl dolls into wardrobes and lifestyles, but otherwise the fantasy world was to be manufactured by the children themselves, not completely manufactured on a video screen. Play value meant that children imagined themselves in the roles of their toys—it intended to teach the child that each of them was capable of driving a car through their world at that speed.

But Mattel and the Handlers brought us more. The history of the toy business is a story of ideas sometimes copied and often improved. In vastly oversimplified terms, such was

Almost from the beginning, Mattel expanded the universe of die-cast cars by offering a variety of products to support its Hot Wheels car line. The Hot Wheels Collector Club appeared in 1970, featuring three chrome-colored muscle cars. The child's Thermos bottle appeared at about the same time, along with a track-trestle kit and a Hot Wheels coloring book.

This is the benchmark Hot Wheels collectible: the rear-loader VW Beach Bomb. The owner of this particular model paid in excess of $66,000 for the car in 2002. Knowledgeable collectors agree that only one model was painted in this pink color.

the introductory chapter in the story of Mattel's two greatest successes, Hot Wheels cars and Barbie dolls. Yet the Hot Wheels story especially deserves a full telling: its birth, its life, its accomplishments, and its successes. From inspiring children to play with toy cars, it has moved full circle. Some of the designers, adults who now work for the world's major automobile manufacturers, grew up playing with Hot Wheels cars. The cars they raced around turns came from the fertile and experienced minds of Harry Bentley Bradley, Ira Gilford, Howard Rees, and Larry Wood, each of them veterans of the full-size auto industry in Detroit, Michigan. Now, in a sweet irony, the cars that some of these new designers have created—Porsche's Boxster, Ferrari's Enzo, Ford's Mustang—have or soon will appear as Hot Wheels models. It is an uncommon story to tell when

the object of the history has inspired others to choose their own careers as a continuation of the fun they had when they were young.

This has been an uncommon history to uncover, revealing equal doses of fascinating characters, creative challenges, financial troubles, and unrivalled successes. There certainly is an element of collectability through the course of these thirty-five years. As baby boomers, we were inspired to want Hot Wheels cars through television advertising. Now we pay astonishing sums to recapture the memories of childhood play. But that is not the greatest significance of this story. What makes the Hot Wheels history worth telling is that these vehicles continue today to form minds, establish self-confidence, and inspire children to imagine who they might become in the years ahead.

1

BEFORE HOT WHEELS CARS:
THE ORIGINS OF MATTEL AND TOY CARS

More new
HOT WHEELS®
cars !
The action
starts here.

When Hot Wheels cars burst onto the scene in the late 1960s, they took the toy car market in a whole new direction. This page from Mattel's 1969 catalog illustrates the color and variety of this exciting new line.

For many decades, centuries even, toy makers have recognized that children like to play with the same things their parents have. Shortly after the first working "motorcars" appeared in the 1880s, toy manufacturers began depicting these new transportation marvels in miniature form. Just as many early automobiles were basically horse buggies fitted with an engine and transmission system, it was a simple design, molding, and manufacturing challenge for toy manufacturers to remove the horse from the front and restyle the molds or stamping presses, giving the toy carriage a motorcar-like front end.

By the middle of the twentieth century, companies such as Corgi, Dinky, Tonka, and others produced a wide variety of toy cars and trucks for kids. The leader in the field was clearly Matchbox, which had first introduced its 1/64th-scale vehicles in 1953. By 1967, while Corgi was selling about 17.5 million cars a year, Matchbox was producing something near 5.5 million models a week. For Elliot and Ruth Handler, it was a target too big to ignore.

In partnership with his friend Harold "Matt" Matson, Elliot had undertaken several entrepreneurial endeavors during the war and postwar eras. Combining their names to create a company identity, Mattel dabbled in everything from discount jewelry to lighting fixtures to picture frames to dollhouse furniture. In 1947 the duo made its first

direct foray into the toy market, and quickly learned some valuable lessons. Mattel came out with the Uke-A-Doodle toy ukulele in January of that year, and it was a smash. But by the time they showed up at the all-important Toy Fair in New York in late February, another company had taken their idea, changed the packaging, and offered it at a lower price. As Elliot explained, "From then on we never introduced a product to the marketplace before the Toy Fair." The experience also taught the Handlers that they had to be sure to make their products unique and truly original, and patentable, so they could not be ripped off so easily.

Matt Matson decided to leave Mattel and Elliot and Ruth bought out his shares in the company. The Handlers' next success, and learning experience, came in 1949 and 1950 with the Futurland Grand Piano. "It was the first toy piano with working black keys," Elliot recalled. "It was a very great success at Toy Fair. We got it out to the market and everybody was happy with it." The trouble, however, was that the aluminum tone bars would break easily during shipping. As a result they received a lot of returns. Not only did this lead Mattel to test the solidity of all its products, but from then on it would test the packaging for its ability to protect its contents.

Before Mattel entered the game, die-cast cars were adult-oriented items. This 1965 Bentley convertible is truly an automobile only an adult would aspire to own. Castings at the time were very crude. Note the seams on the front and rear fenders.

The casting quality of this Japanese model was excellent, with detail clear on the car's side badge, the passenger compartment air vents, and the side door handles. Still, it was not a model that inspired children to get down on the floor and play.

When Mattel began exploring the competition in the die-cast car world, these are the types of cars they found: a Cadillac sedan (blue), Toyota Corona sedan, Ford (black top) two-door coupe, Mercedes-Benz sedan, Bentley convertible, and VW Karmann Ghia hardtop. The detail was minimal and the colors were drab.

For Ruth and Elliot, a basic requirement of any good toy was participation, a concept they called "play value." This applied to the musical toys they developed early on, and it became the overriding principle when they started down the road of die-cast cars. At that time, die-cast cars were not considered toys by Mattel or by the industry. They were a hobby item, lacking that all-important play value. They were sold in hobby stores, not toy stores, and usually in a glass case. They didn't "do" anything. Not yet, anyway.

In a few short decades, Mattel had grown into a company with sales in excess of $100 million. During the 1950s, before Hot Wheels cars were even a glimmer in Elliot's eye, Mattel was best known for making toy guns: the Fanner 50, the Burp Gun, the Winchester Repeating Rifle, the Shootin' Shell toys, the belt buckle Derringer, the Marauder M-16 rifle. Boys who watched such popular television shows as *Gunsmoke* and *The Life and Legend of Wyatt Earp* saw Mattel's toy guns advertised on TV, and soon they had them in their rooms.

The toy gun phenomenon started to slow down in the early 1960s, and the assassination of President John F. Kennedy in November 1963 further sparked the anti-gun movement in America. "Gun sales were dropping off," Elliot recalled, "and customers, parents, teachers, and others were going against guns. We needed an inexpensive boys' toy, just like Barbie was, at that time, a low-priced girls' toy. I was trying to figure out where to go." Parts of their toy guns were made from die-cast metal, so Mattel began looking for a new category in which they could take advantage of that expertise.

The story of how Elliot Handler was spurred to pursue toy cars goes like this, according to Harry Bentley Bradley, a designer at Mattel starting in 1966: Elliot and Ruth were visiting one of their children, either Barbara or Ken, and one of the grandkids was playing with die-cast cars. "Elliot basically thought, 'I have a grandchild of mine playing with a toy that I don't even compete with!'"

Miniature cars were not an easy sale to Mattel's executives, however. Elliot set his marketing department to work researching the current state of affairs in the toy-car market. They came back with a report saying it was a bad idea for Mattel to go into die-cast cars, a good way to lose a lot of money. Mattel was too late getting into the marketplace, they told him. Matchbox from England was too strong, their sales too high. Yet Elliot Handler believed in the viability of his idea as strongly as his wife Ruth had pushed for her Barbie doll a decade earlier.

Jack Malek came on board at Mattel in 1964 as a general project engineer. He was the program manager for Barbie and Walking Barbie when Elliot brought his new idea to the Product Committee, which met once a week to discuss the progress of various items. "Elliot came in with a Matchbox model and said, 'Why don't we make something like this?'" Malek recalled. "He got a long dissertation from the marketing manager about how the market was overloaded, there were already too many types of little cars out there, and there was no reason to believe ours would sell.

"So Elliot listened, and when the meeting was over, he walked to the door, turned around and said, 'Well, let's make it anyway.'"

2

WHERE'S THE SHTICK?
WHERE'S THE PIZZAZZ?

Collectors debate whether the Custom Mustang or the Custom Camaro came first, but both first appeared with the launch of Hot Wheels cars in mid-1968. The bright colors, metallic light blue in the case of the Custom Mustang, and hood scoops helped give Hot Wheels cars their distinctive look.

There is an axiom that suggests that success has many fathers while failure is a bastard. Nowhere is that statement more true than at Mattel during the birth of Hot Wheels cars. Perhaps as many as a half-dozen designers, engineers, and model makers created their own versions of a Matchbox car that had play value. Elliot Handler favored a system of friendly competition to solve problems, setting multiple people and even multiple departments to work in pursuit of the same goal. This same belief in friendly competition to inspire creativity was part of Jack Ryan's management technique as well.

Before coming to Mattel, Ryan had been an electronics engineer with Raytheon. According to many people, he was an outright genius. Raytheon had named Ryan project supervisor for its U.S. Navy Sparrow missile program when he was just twenty-eight. When he first met the Handlers, Ryan proposed that if Mattel wanted to grow big, the Handlers should take him on as a consultant. He would take no salary and only accept a 1.5 percent royalty on any toy he or his staff brought into production. In the early days, it was a golden deal for the Handlers; in later years, it proved platinum for Ryan.

Ryan ran Mattel's Preliminary Design department, a creative assembly of about eighty artists, designers, engineers, and fabricators. From the start, when Elliot had asked Jack about taking on Matchbox, Jack had not limited himself by assigning the task to a favored engineer. He asked

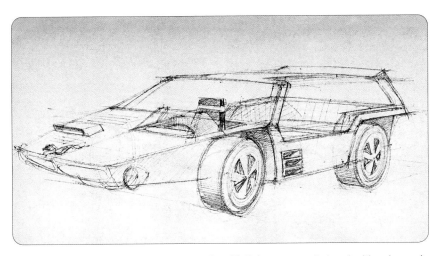

By its second year of Hot Wheels production, Mattel was overwhelmed with sales and was looking for new product ideas. It farmed out a great deal of wood modeling to an outside firm, Industrial Design Affiliates, which also took on a design role. IDA introduced this "chauffeur-driven town car."

Industrial Design Affiliates created numerous Hot Wheels ideas in 1969 and into the 1970s. They designed and proposed this helicopter-car in October 1969, though it was never produced.

many of his staff to work on the project—a fact that leads to modern-day confusion in charting the origination of the cars.

As Handler and Ryan set creative forces in motion to come up with a new product that could compete in the die-cast car market, marketing pressed ahead with its studies. "Elliot Handler wants us to look at these, okay, so be it," Fred Adickes recalled. Adickes was hired in 1963 to establish an industrial design discipline within Mattel. "John Kensey, in the marketing department, did some child testing. They noted that the kids drove the toy cars up and down their corduroy pants legs and their chest and belly and arms, and sometimes the kids would go 'vroom, vroommmm.' They did seem to enjoy having them to hold and cherish and put in their pocket."

"I can remember personally being very skeptical of this," John Kensey said. "To me, they were just little cars like I used to play with. I didn't get it. I felt that Mattel was way too late getting into this, that we just shouldn't do it."

Walter Ross, Kensey's boss, disagreed. Ross had been hired to establish a product planning department, largely at Jack Ryan's recommendation. "Ryan was brilliant, unbelievably diversified, and he would be willing to consider developing anything." Ross said. "But he was also interested in establishing a discipline that would qualify and quantify the efficacy of new products coming out of his Preliminary Design labs. And I thought going into the

die-cast toy market was a good idea." That was because Ross already understood from Ryan how wisely and carefully Elliot and Ruth worked.

With Ross in place as a supporter, Elliot's next step was to bring in someone who knew cars and could give them some ideas. Fred Adickes had managed Chrysler's Styling Engineering department before coming to Mattel, and he knew how to talk to car people. He got the assignment to return to Detroit in late September 1966. He advertised for automotive designers in the *Detroit*

As Industrial Design Affiliates worked its way through the model-making process, it developed blueprints of concepts it and Hot Wheels designers had created. This drawing dates from 1969, but Mattel didn't introduce this six-wheeler until a decade later, when it released the Space Van in 1979.

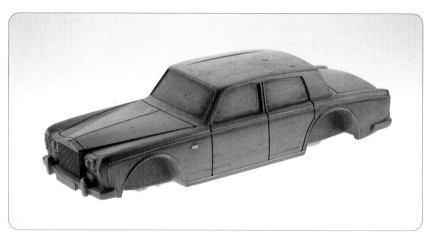

It was a curious decision to produce a distinctly British ultra-luxury automobile as a second-year Hot Wheels model. Perhaps Elliot Handler meant to demonstrate to rival Matchbox that the American upstart could even do English cars better, and certainly make them go faster. This epoxy block casting represents the Rolls-Royce Silver Shadow, introduced in 1969.

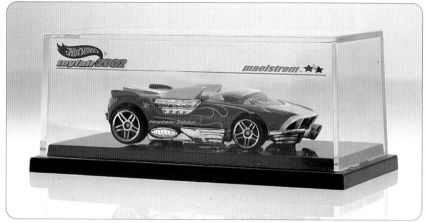

Designers at Mattel have always gone above and beyond the call of duty. For Toy Fair 2001, Hot Wheels designers prepared specially painted and decorated Maelstrom models as gifts to their customers. This concept racer appeared later in the year in a regular blisterpack, introduced as #12 in the 2001 First Editions.

Free Press, and the small classified ad had included Mattel's name and its location in California. It generated great interest, but not for the reasons Mattel hoped.

Harry Bentley Bradley was Adickes' second interview at Cadillac. "To fellows in their twenties or thirties who were complete car fanatics," Bradley recalled, "Mattel didn't have any meaning. But there was a real passion on the part of Detroit designers to come to California, because the Japanese were coming into the United States with these grotesque little cars. The quality was high, the fuel economy was excellent, but they were pretty strange looking. A lot of us believed if you could come to California where the Japanese had set up headquarters, you could start a pretty good business doing design consulting to these companies. I wasn't interested in this job initially, but the more I helped other designers prepare their portfolios, I thought this might be something very worthwhile." Two years earlier, Bradley's portfolio had gotten him admitted to Stanford University on a full GM Fellowship for a master's degree in engineering. He showed his drawings to Adickes and got the job.

"I had a reputation at General Motors for my renderings. I put hot rods and exciting cars in them, whereas most of the fellows did renderings that simply showed the vehicle they were designing. And I could draw girls just about as well as anybody in America at the time, so I always had these gorgeous girls with tiny vinyl skirts and high boots and heavy eyeliner." Adickes told Bradley to report for work in early October 1966.

After several years designing Cadillacs, Chevrolets, and Pontiacs in the elegant Eero Saarinen–designed GM Tech Center campus, Bradley was horrified by the modest Mattel buildings when he drove up in his chromed, school bus yellow El Camino. Some people at Mattel were probably equally horrified by Bradley's vehicle. Bradley had bought the pickup truck new before going to Stanford in 1964, and after his year in grad school, he returned to Detroit and asked his friends, legendary car builders Mike and Larry Alexander, to lower the roofline slightly and graft on the roofline of a 1963 Pontiac Grand Prix,

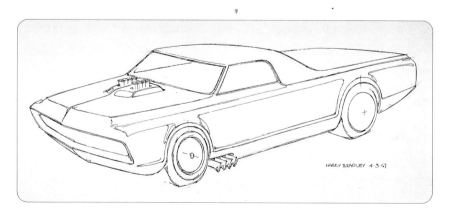

Through months of uncertainty about what he was supposed to be doing at Mattel, Harry Bradley had the answer right under his nose. His personal transportation, a modified Chevrolet El Camino pickup, would come to represent the unique Hot Wheels style.

with its sweeping concave rear window. He wanted them to mount fat Firestone Redline tires on American Racing five-spoke mag wheels. The Alexander brothers covered the roof and cargo bed tonneau cover in padded black Morokhide, the same vinyl covering material that Cadillac used on its Fleetwood sedans and limousines. Bradley had earlier designed a "power dome" front hood for Mike and Larry to sell in their retail parts business. He asked the Alexanders to mount one on his truck, and to this Bradley added a set of eight flared aluminum drink cups, sanded, polished, and inset into the hood to resemble fuel injector stacks.

"So," Bradley continued, "I pulled up in front of Mattel in this wild-looking truck. At the time, hot rodding and customizing in America had taken a real downturn, especially in California. When I grew up in La Jolla, I used to see chopped Mercs and '32 roadsters a lot, but in the 1960s, it was VW beetles and Combi-Vans with flowers and peace signs painted all over them."

Even after he got there, Bradley had no idea why Mattel wanted a car designer. "Nobody seemed to know why I was there," he said, "but everyone was great to me, fascinated by my background in the auto industry." Bradley had suffered polio as a child, and to this day he walks

Once Harry Bradley began giving the cars in his designs new twists like dramatic roof lines and exaggerated wheels, he took die-cast cars to a whole new level. Bowtie loyalists maintain that the Custom Camaro, shown here in metallic yellow, was the first of the Hot Wheels line.

with crutches. "They gave me a parking space right in front of the building with the other executives because of my disability, and of course my blazing yellow El Camino was parked right alongside the big new 1966 Cadillacs I'd designed three years earlier."

Adickes showed Bradley to his drawing board and then told him why he was there. Elliot Handler wanted to get into small die-cast cars.

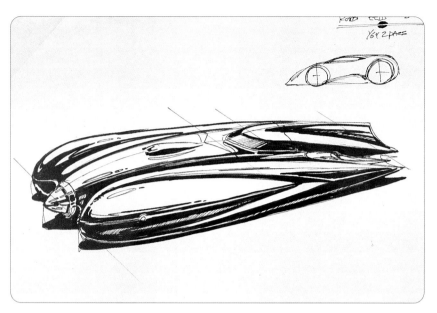

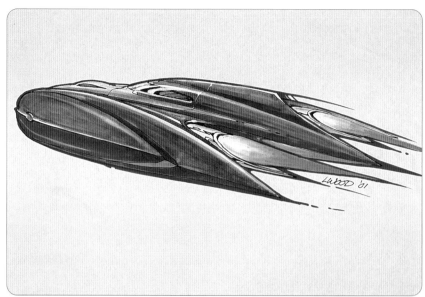

This pen-and-ink sketch of a land-speed-record car sprang from Larry Wood's fertile imagination. It featured a nose treatment that suggested it was jet or rocket propelled. The idea grew from there.

After sketching out the design for his land-speed concept racer, Wood had to give it power. For Wood, an enthusiastic hot-rod builder, a body this sleek required something more than just a supercharged V-8 or even a V-16 engine. For Wood, this meant jets with afterburners, or rockets.

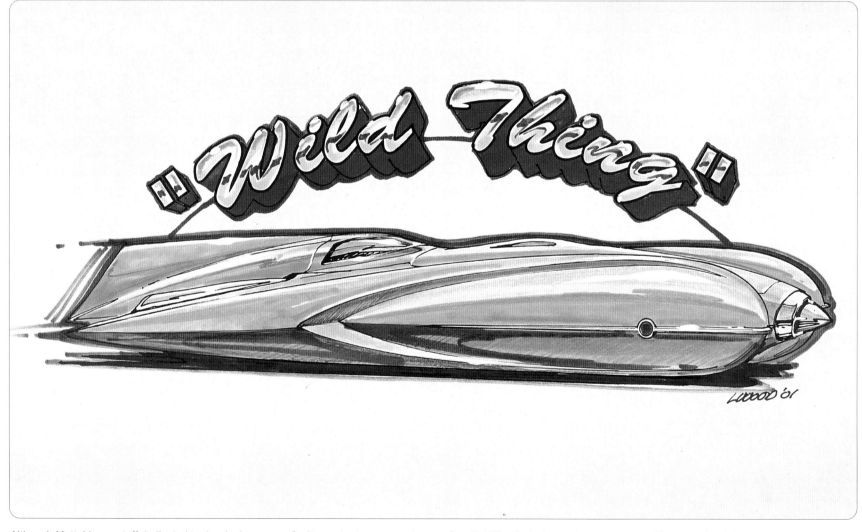

Although Mattel has a staff dedicated to developing names for its products, more and more often Hot Wheels designers have come up with names for their own works. Larry Wood decided to call his sleek, jet-powered racer the Wild Thing, and it went into production under that name in 2003.

Presenting the sizzling *HOT WHEELS*® *SUPER-CHARGER,*™ perpetual power boost for all *HOT WHEELS*® CARS!

All *HOT WHEELS SUPER-CHARGERS* operate on 2 D batteries (not included).

Mattel introduced the Super-Charger for 1969. As this device went through testing and development, Hot Wheels designers and engineers found they had to revise the design and balance of a number of vehicles. This Super-Charger, with its rapidly counter-spinning padded wheels, accelerated Hot Wheels cars to near top speed. Narrow vehicles, such as the open-wheel Grand Prix series race cars and the earliest versions of the VW Beach Bomb surfer van, got twisted coming through the wheels and flew off the track. Engineering invented side pods for the racers and redesigned the Beach Bomb, mounting the surfboards along the sides.

For many years, Mattel resisted issuing its Hot Wheels cars in pink. Some said this was a "Barbie color" forced onto a boy's toy. Still, according to Bob Rosas, engineering and design tested the color on many models. Of these, Mattel produced the pink 1990 "California Custom" Baja Bug (far left). Neither the pink 1975 Monza 2+2 nor the pink 1978 Corvette Stingray ever appeared on the shelves. The '57 T-Bird did show up in a pink-red color for a Kmart set in 2001.

"I never liked little cars," Bradley recalled. "I just love the big stuff, the real stuff. I had no affinity for small model cars. 'So how do we do that?' I asked."

"We're going to go to toy stores and buy every die-cast car we can find!" Adickes replied.

"Actually, we did that," Len Mayem said with a laugh, picking up the story. Mayem worked in the marketing department at Mattel, and providing this kind of input was a marketing job. "We did buy them all, but there weren't that many to buy, not even a couple hundred. And they were all quite primitive, the paints were not exciting, the detail was crude." At that time, Matchbox was Mattel's biggest competitor. It had just put in a new $100,000 electrostatic painting system that efficiently did the entire car in one color. But the color choices still seemed drab.

Mayem and Adickes mounted the cars on low three-by-four-foot rolling upright display boards. They attached the cars horizontally, dozens on each board, with the passenger side wired onto the board so Bradley could see the driver's sides fully.

"It became a bit of an intrusion into the department," Bradley said. "These boards were all over the place with these cars on them. And some of them were really horrible. The state of die-cast cars in those days was not very good. A lot of them were utterly boring Humber Hawks, Simcas, Ford Prefects. There was no spirit to them whatsoever."

Worse than that, no one yet had any idea what Bradley was supposed to do. He had yet to start a single drawing.

"My boss was Gerry Schmidt, the lead designer, a remarkably talented and intelligent man who had this quiet smile on his face. He looked at me after a few days and said, 'You're on your own. I've nothing to offer you. Good luck.'"

So Bradley started doing renderings of futuristic cars, hoping that's what they were looking for. "Something like what I thought a 1984 car would look like back in 1966. Elliot would come by regularly and he seemed absolutely fascinated with my drawing technique. The other four designers used markers, and they did really functional drawings of little children playing with objects. These were like product design drawings where you show how one piece fits inside another, that the batteries go here, the motor fits there.

"And here I was doing these advanced concepts, sleek, low, wild-looking cars with tall women standing next to them in gorgeous evening gowns with maybe a street rod in the background." He laughed. "The other designers used B-sheets, 11- by 17-inch pages. I was drawing on 18-by-24s, and I was used to drawing real cars full size on papers the size of a wall."

Elliot was fascinated, but as Bradley soon learned, it was not a warm admiration. Handler objected to the size of paper Bradley was using, the special chalks and fixatives, the fact that he spent days or as much as a week on each drawing, and that the finished presentation on black boards required four or five sheets behind the actual rendering to obscure the black. It was the way things were done at GM, but Handler told Bradley that it was too wasteful. Elliot asked him to just make quick sketches and put them on the end of his drawing boards as the other designers did, so as Elliot walked by, he could take a quick look.

"And I think these futuristic cars don't have much meaning," Bradley remembered Elliot telling him. "They're kind of dream cars. Let's stay closer to home." Bradley was startled and wondered if he'd made a mistake taking this job.

"I didn't know how to draw a car that looked like you took a picture with your Kodak camera. The whole idea at GM was to make these things look really exotic. We automatically made everything look a little lower and wider. I kept wondering why we didn't just go down to the local Chevy dealer and get their brochures."

Nevertheless, Bradley began drawing cars that looked like 1967 Ford Mustangs and Pontiac GTOs. Even with that, Elliot still was not satisfied. The rearview mirrors, license plates, and door handles would not reduce to a small scale. "Don't do that either," Elliot told his designer. Bradley learned that for reduced scale die-cast cars he needed to enlarge door gaps and other intentional openings so they'd hold the reduction.

"My drawings made these cars look like they were done by Betty Crocker. They all had a kind of baked quality to them because those door gaps were not crisp, they were rounded."

"Well, gee, we're not really keen on this either," he heard Elliot say. All around him, other executives were saying things like this to him, too, being very polite, meaning well, but unable to articulate what they did want. His new friends in design, too, were wondering what he was doing there, what was going on there.

Then Les Estrain's market research department voiced its findings. If Mattel was going to do what Matchbox was doing, it should not go into die-cast miniature cars. Unless Mattel could introduce some "play value" to make these cars into toys, this was a guaranteed way to lose a lot of money.

Not far away, in Jack Barcus' Research and Design department, the designers and engineers heard the silence these matters provoked. One of those engineers was Bill Summerfield.

"The question came down to us, 'What can we do to make this something different?'" Summerfield recalled. "The expression they used was, 'What's the shtick in this?' They meant, how do we give this thing some pizzazz? How do we give it play value?"

3

CARS LIKE THAT THING YOU DRIVE

Harry Bradley's modified El Camino pickup inspired Elliot Handler, who told his new designer that he wanted his die-cast miniature cars to be modified "like that thing of yours outside." Handler authorized production of Bradley's El Camino as the Custom Fleetside for 1968.

Howard Newman had been with Mattel as a mechanical engineer for three years by the time Harry Bradley arrived. Newman had learned quickly how the toy business worked and about its constant hunger for new ideas. It was an industry rule-of-thumb that a toy had to pay for itself in its first year because many of them barely lasted that long. Anything that ran into a second year was pure gravy for the profit-and-loss statement. Most toy companies figured half or more of their product lineup had to be replaced each year.

By the mid-1960s, Mattel already had established its place in the industry in America. What Newman saw was a company that liked to come up with great ideas and invest very heavily in them in the way of tooling and know-how, molds, and marketing strategies so that in the interval between late winter's Toy Fair and September, when they were shipped, the new toys couldn't be knocked off.

"They knew what they were doing and they hired very aggressively," Newman explained. "Ruth Handler was, if nothing else, a very aggressive person. She sent her recruiters out to find engineers or designers and she told them to do whatever they had to do to get them."

The rules at Mattel were very fluid. Designers and engineers were encouraged to shoot down ideas, hold things up to question,

Mattel's designers and engineers constantly experimented with adding tricks and special features to Hot Wheels cars. One such experiment was the Hot Wheels "sound machine," in which the cars made engine noises as they rolled. As the wheels and axles rotated, a magnetic audio tape band ran through a tiny resonator box. Derek Gable and a few other engineers worked on this idea beginning in the late 1960s and continuing into the 1970s.

Derek Gable fitted the prototype sound machine brass chassis to the Custom Continental. Engineers routinely selected the 1969 Custom Continental for prototype development because it was one of the largest Hot Wheels models. Here you can see the tiny "audio" pickup wand, just between the front wheels, that read impulses off the magnetic stripe tape between the axles. The white structure inside the car amplified and clarified the sound.

Another variation of the engine sound strip used raised elements on the sound ribbon to create a vroom-vroom-vroom sound. Sound cars never reached production. Mattel rejected them because of high production costs and because the cars ran noticeably slower than regular Hot Wheels cars.

Elliot Handler wanted Harry Bradley to draw something that looked like Bradley's modified El Camino pickup. He understood then what Elliot wanted, and designs began to pour off Bradley's drawing board. This drawing, prepared by Bradley for a Hot Wheels collector gathering in 2001, illustrates this early piece of Hot Wheels history. Bradley's 1964 Chevrolet El Camino pickup is in the lower left, with a drawing of the 1968 Hot Wheels Custom Fleetside on the lower right. Note the distinctive Redline tires and five-spoke wheels on Bradley's truck.

criticize their superiors, and be competitive. When the company thought about going into a product, it launched a bunch of market research and produced summaries, charts, and reports that detailed how many of what was sold by what company in what years at what prices. These tactics were successful, and Elliot and Ruth approved the creation of a toy category called Small Cars.

"One of the first projects I worked on was something someone else had begun," Newman recalled, "something that made a motor sound. They asked me to develop the motor sound element, to use it in a toy. I designed an Indy-style racer with that motor sound device in it. It was about a foot long, very durable. It was the classic push toy, something even a two-year-old could operate. The friction between the tires and floor wound up a rotating weight—there was a flywheel in there—and when the kid released it, the car took off and ran a little ways. My Indy racer sounded like a souped-up eight-cylinder Chevy."

Switch 'N' Go cars followed the success of that project. These cars were five inches long and were electrically driven with a hidden guide wheel that followed a tube. Children operated switches and cross-overs were directed remotely by blowing air into the tubing.

Newman then was assigned to work with Jack Ryan on the Small Cars project. It was a cross between a very detailed Matchbox car and a slot car. A pin stuck down from the car and rode in the track's slot.

"Somehow I was to try to get a cross-breed and get it going. I worked on it for Ryan for quite a while and it didn't do anything. It just wasn't a good enough idea," Newman recalled.

Down the hall from Newman, Harry Bradley was beginning to wonder if he had any ideas at all. The marketing questions were not going away: Where was the play value? Where was the shelf space?

"I'd never heard of this before. At GM if we wanted to introduce a new car, by God, we'd just introduce it. But I learned that retail stores only have so much shelf space for Mattel products. If Mattel wanted its top-of-the-line, best selling items in those spaces, they shouldn't bring out the little cars unless something else went out. The marketing people were quite upset about this. 'We can't do this,' they kept saying. But Elliot was the co-founder and president and he never wavered. He was very even mannered, even in the face of vigorous opposition."

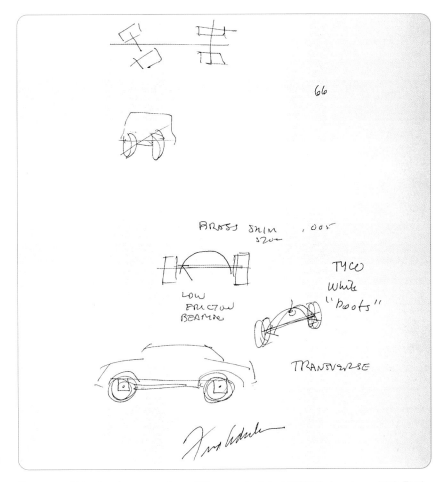

Every great idea begins somewhere. This vaguely dated (1966?) drawing, which Fred Adickes later signed, is probably among the earliest illustrations of the processes that went into the development of Mattel's die-cast cars. Adickes' concept was for a car that might be steerable. He thought the wheels might turn on a "low-friction beam," suspended by a 0.005-inch brass shim.

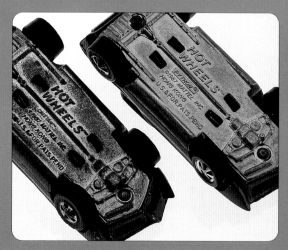

Creative names have continued throughout the 35 years of Hot Wheels cars. Carol Robinson, successor to Alexandra Laird as the Hot Wheels "naming lady," came up with names like King 'Kuda, Light My Firebird, and Sugar Caddy to describe the Plymouth Barracuda, Pontiac Firebird, and Cadillac Eldorado in the 1970 Spoilers series. This souped-up Mercury Cougar, also introduced in 1970, is known as the Nitty Gritty Kitty.

What's in a name? Well, Mattel found out when it planned to introduce its Cheetah in 1968. As it turned out, this was the same name that GM executive Bill Thomas had bestowed, and registered, on his Corvette-powered racer. Mattel produced only a handful of Cheetah bases before renaming it the Python.

WHAT'S IN A NAME?

A variety of legends have arisen suggesting that a name for Mattel's exciting new car project rolled off of Elliot Handler's tongue in a flash of inspiration. The most popular version reports that he christened the little cars "hot wheels" immediately after first seeing them roll along the hallway outside Fred Adickes' office. "That's one set of hot wheels you've got there," he reportedly said. Elliot Handler is certainly brilliant, but he admits that his strength is in ideas, not in words and names. For that, he recalled, he looked to Mattel's packaging department. The packaging department had someone whose job it was to make up product names. Inside Mattel, they called Alexandra Laird "the Namesmith."

Mattel did all its creative work in-house and came up with the copy for advertising, the text for catalogs, scripts and storyboards for commercials, and the names for toys. At Mattel, Laird was the one-person copywriting staff. She named every Barbie doll costume, every cap pistol, and every pre-school building block set from her arrival in 1964.

"In those days, Mattel didn't allow women in their product meetings," Laird recalled. "I had to get second-hand whatever the powers-that-be said they wanted. This information came from my boss, Marvin Barab." Laird would be told to go see an engineer or a designer in R&D or Preliminary Design, behind closed doors, to discuss a particular product.

"So one day Marvin told me that Mattel was going after a piece of the action that Matchbox cars had. They had come up with these little cars. He told me to go back to R&D to see the cars they were working on, the little cars with the big wheels. Mattel had never done anything like these before and they had no names, no logo. This was just an idea they were working on. I went back and looked at these funny little cars and then wrote a whole bunch of names on a list the way I always did. I thought about the cars and pulled out my thesaurus. I had three children and I was aware of the street lingo, that cars were referred to as 'wheels.' I was just trying to find a gimmick to hang my hat on here. I kept looking at these wheels."

At the top of the list that Alex handed to Elliot, she had written "Big Wheels." Laird continued: "Elliot

looked at it, half-smiled, and asked me for another word, different from 'big.' He talked about the California Custom styling and wondered aloud if that was what people would call 'hot?' Hot Wheels?" Elliott and Alex bounced some more names off each other, but they kept going back to Elliott's suggestion—Hot Wheels.

Later, Harry Bradley went into Jack Ryan's office for a meeting. He had nearly completed an entire line of cars Mattel could produce in its first year. He had drawn a Camaro, a Mustang, a Cougar, a Firebird, and others, all in a style and presentation format clearly in Mattel's "groove."

"Jack had this quiet, nasally voice," Bradley explained. "That day he announced to me that Mattel had decided to call these cars Hot Wheels. I thought that was a terrible name. I was pretty inflexible at the time. 'Hot rod' was a holy, divine name. Hot rod! It's America's purest automotive form. Hot Wheels struck me as awkward and inappropriate, and I said, 'Oh, that's ridiculous, Jack.'

"Well, then I thought about it some more, and I knew it was a stroke of genius. It *was* perfect."

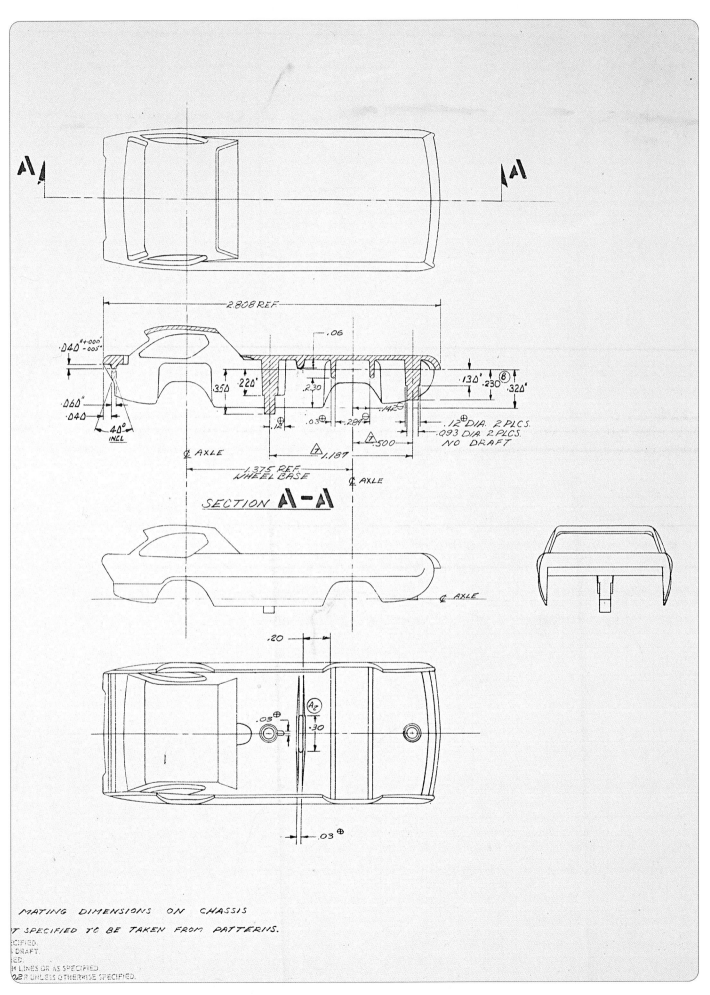

From Fred Adickes' rough concept sketch from 1966, it wasn't long until detailed engineering scale drawings of Harry Bradley's custom Dodge Deora were made. Built on a 1.375-inch wheelbase, the Deora measured 2.808 inches long overall. It was introduced into the Hot Wheels line in 1968.

During an impromptu meeting with Elliot Handler, Harry Bradley took his preliminary sketches of a Plymouth Barracuda and used it as a note pad. He listed military vehicles, sports cars, and vans that Handler envisioned as subsequent offerings.

Once Harry Bradley understood what Elliot Handler wanted in car "design," he quickly produced modified cars that resembled his own personal vehicle. This is Bradley's rendering of what became the Custom Cougar.

Jack Malek joined Mattel in 1964 to be a general project engineer for Jack Ryan. His first assignment had been one of personal interest to Ryan, who was a music lover and frustrated musician. Ryan wanted a self-tuning guitar. Malek learned that this required strings of a specific diameter when the guitar was manufactured so they wouldn't have to be tuned. Ryan approved the order for the first string, the E string, a mandolin wire from Driver-Harris in New Jersey. When Malek and Ryan priced out the instrument with its expensive wire, it had a selling price that was far too high for the market in 1965, so Mattel killed the project and Malek's wire went into storage.

Malek moved up at Mattel and enjoyed several promotions for his hard work. By 1966, while serving on the Product Committee,

Harry Bradley's rendering of what became the Custom Camaro included rough sketches of line placement for the Redline tires. Bradley gave most of his cars "power bulges" on the hood and exhaust pipes sticking out from the body.

Malek and the others were facing the challenge of trying to come up with a way to make Mattel's new die-cast cars stand apart from the competition.

"It was about 3:30 in the afternoon and we sat in there until about 10 o'clock that night, thinking of various alternatives to making something that would be unique and different. The basic concept was to make a small car. The Matchbox car was about two inches long, and it sat on axles about one-eighth of an inch in diameter, staked on both ends. And it sat. You had to push it in order to make it roll along.

"I happened to mention that I had these ten thousand feet of precision wire used for mandolin strings, which was extremely strong and could bend around itself. If you made an axle with a little tiny wire like that, you'd have a very fast turning, low-friction system."

Meanwhile up on the third floor, as Harry Bradley labored away, Handler walked up to his drawing table and looked at what he'd sketched.

"You know what, Harry?" Bradley remembered Elliot telling him. "I want these cars to look like that thing of yours outside."

Bradley was crushed. "He spoke about my El Camino exactly the way grown people speak about hot rods and custom cars—with less than real approval. Even though my El Camino was a beautifully crafted piece, and driving it down the street was a little like the circus coming to town, he still called it 'that thing of yours.'

"But, everything I had gone through, learning to draw and communicate in the Mattel manner, 'getting in the Mattel groove,' they called it, and coming to understand these die-cast cars, well, all of the sudden I could make it apply! I started doing new 1967 Camaros and Mustangs, Firebirds and Thunderbirds, Cougars and Cadillacs, all of them very much 'like' my El Camino."

Over the next few days, as Bradley drew, Elliot began to enumerate the elements that would define the cars. First, he wanted very bright strong colors, candy colors. He didn't know how they'd accomplish it, but he wanted vivid colors.

Next, he wanted that "power statement" on the hood, something to suggest there was high horsepower underneath it, like

The designers in the 1960s never predicted how popular the Hot Wheels cars would be. In 1970, Mattel licensed Ken Snyder Properties to create and distribute a Hot Wheels jigsaw puzzle.

One of Elliot Handler's prime directives for the new line of die-cast car toys was that they had to have "custom California style" and a "hot rod rake." To Handler this meant rear tires that were larger than the fronts, and the car's rear end jacked up higher than the front. This Matchbox Mustang was mounted on a handmade chassis to illustrate such qualities.

Bradley's power dome. Bradley took that further and left several of the engines exposed altogether.

Elliot thought Bradley's five-spoke wheels with little chromed nuts really gave his truck personality, and he liked the red-striped tires. Elliot already had seen them on Mustangs and other muscle cars, but thought they were amazing on bright-colored cars, like Bradley's El Camino. Elliot also wanted the roofline of the El Camino to appear on the little cars.

The battles were far from over, however. As far as marketing was concerned, the car still failed. Even though they had made them look shiny and attractive, so what? You still couldn't play with them, and marketing was not going to clear the shelves of something that was already selling. The legal department also had not let up on its worries of reproducing someone else's car without permission.

All the while, the cast of characters was growing in this effort to make Elliot's little cars come to life. Market research resumed child testing in half-hour sessions with kids from local-area schools.

Mattel was able to attract more and more creative designers as it established a Hot Wheels identity. This design for the Whip Creamer concept car, introduced in 1970, came from the desk of Paul Tam.

Rita Rao was one of a group of child psychologists Mattel had on staff to run and monitor these tests. "Once we introduced the children to the toys and told them what they could or shouldn't do," Rao said, "I'd tell the kids I had to go back to my desk and do some work, that I'd be back in fifteen or twenty minutes to see how they were doing. Then we'd go behind the one-way mirrors and watch what they did and listen to what they said." While the testers pretty much worked with any toy that came along, they tested nearly all the products for their appeal. A lot of them were tested as well for what Rao called "can do," which means at what ages can the children actually do what the toy was intended to do. With cars it was easy; they brought in pairs or groups of boys or girls and let them push cars across the carpet.

"At the end of those sessions, we'd let the children pick out one of the toys to take home." That's when the best lessons often were learned.

Floyd Schlau, an engineer in product development, took notes one day while child researcher Rosemary Kazlow ushered in group after group of children, all given the chance to play with small cars and trucks. Kazlow and Schlau watched and tried to understand what kids liked, to see if there was a pattern. Did they like commercial trucks or emergency vehicles, or did colorful cars do it for them?

"We'd always ask the kids afterwards, sort of like an exit interview, which car would you like to take home with you?" Schlau explained. "That's where it came out this one day. This one little boy said he wanted to take home a little blue Chevy sedan.

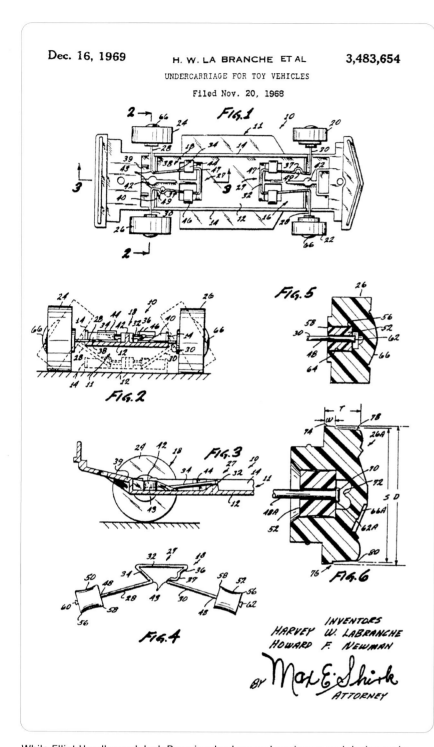

Dec. 16, 1969   H. W. LA BRANCHE ET AL   3,483,654

UNDERCARRIAGE FOR TOY VEHICLES

Filed Nov. 20, 1968

FIG. 1

FIG. 2

FIG. 3

FIG. 4

FIG. 5

FIG. 6

INVENTORS
HARVEY W. LABRANCHE
HOWARD F. NEWMAN

BY Max E. Shirk
ATTORNEY

While Elliot Handler and Jack Ryan involved several engineers and designers in creating Mattel's first miniature die-cast cars, engineer Howard Newman gets credit for developing and improving the cars' independent suspension and their quick-turning wheels. Newman's initial system attached four individual z-shaped mandolin-wire axles to each car chassis. However, this allowed too much opportunity for inaccurate axle placement, which caused the cars to roll slowly or to veer to one side or the other. This drawing shows Newman's improved two-axle system. It also shows construction of the free-rolling wheel itself. The secret of its speed was the inner Delrin bearing. Mattel surrounded the Delrin with a nylon wheel. Mattel's patent attorney filed the application in November 1968 during the first year of Hot Wheels.

"Now that was a little odd," Schlau continued. "We had fire engines, trucks of every kind, all sorts of glittery chrome and bright colors, but this dark blue sedan made it."

When asked why he preferred the sedan, the little boy replied, "Because it rolls."

"That was it," Schlau recalled. "The car invented itself."

In fact, it was not quite so simple as that. Elliot and Ruth unleashed an assortment of engineers to make toy cars roll. They devised two separate product concept and design departments, Jack Barcus' R&D group and Ryan's Preliminary Design, in pursuit of this goal.

Fred Adickes, Mattel's chief of industrial design, got the word from Schlau in product planning and from John Kensey and Walt Ross in marketing that this was what kids do. Having toy cars that rolled was part of the Handlers' philosophy that toys are tools for children to learn to be adults, and realism was a fairly dependable criterion.

"In our dolls," Adickes said, "we made them as realistic as possible. We made Barbie doll's knees bend, we gave babies puffy soft cheeks, we made guns as realistic as we could. Coming from Detroit, I sketched out a brass shim-stock straight transverse leaf front and rear axle. We had these slot cars with white rear wheels that were nicely round, made by Tyco. They called them 'White Boots.' Though the front of the car dragged on its pin, it didn't roll."

Jack DeGelder was a model maker. Adickes handed him the sketches and told him to grab any toy car body and see what he could do. Before the end of the day, he brought the car back.

"He set it on the table and it kind of bounced, and it rolled at the same time. My desk wasn't level and it started to roll on its own. I thought, this is neat."

Adickes had gone through the Indian Guides program with his son Zack, and together they participated in the pine block derby. It occurred to Adickes that this car could run by gravity. That night on the way home from work he stopped at a hardware store and picked up a double garage door weather strip. It was wide enough to fit the car and had a flat portion nestled between two raised edges. At home that night, he handed the car to Zack and together they gave it its first child tests and rolled it across the floor.

The interior of this unpainted Custom T-Bird shows the first version of the independent suspension that Mattel engineers devised to allow the Hot Wheels cars to go fast and make it through banked turns and tight loops. Each of the four axles, formed into a Z shape, are independently staked in place. Quality-control issues eventually led to the abandonment of the z-shaped axle for the simpler and more reliable straight axle.

The next day, using a c-clamp from his own garage, Adickes cinched the weather strip onto a low shelf in his office and pointed the long strip out his door and down the hallway. He let the car go. It shot along the track and down the hall. As he prepared to release it for its second run, Elliot walked by on his morning rounds through Preliminary Design.

"I hadn't even had the chance to show this to my boss, Jack Ryan, but I let it roll for Elliot. Again it shot down the hallway, but this time I lost it. By the time I found it and got back, Jack was there beside Elliot and they both agreed this was what they wanted the car to do. Together Elliot and Jack coined the name the American Series, probably just to contrast it to the English Matchbox I was using for a body to show off the running gear."

Elliot Handler's system of friendly competition meant that he and Jack Ryan circulated among the creative minds in design and engineering like bees cross-pollinating flowers. Handler and Ryan picked up an idea here and deposited it there. They took Malek's mandolin wire and spread it through the department. They absorbed Adickes' idea to adopt Tyco's white boot wheels and passed it on to others. This technique sometimes minimized the time others wasted to reach identical solutions and it greatly accelerated new toy development. In other instances, duplicated efforts and parallel developments led to quantum leaps in product sophistication.

At almost the same time that Elliot and Jack watched Adickes' car roll down the hallway, engineer Howard Newman

The Custom Cougar was a popular model in the inaugural year of Hot Wheels cars in 1968. Its bulging hood scoop and high-riding stance were reflective of muscle car modifications one would find cruising the streets of 1960s America.

was reaching a similar, if more complex solution to the question of free-rolling. After the slot car cross-breed failed, he worked on his own to find other car ideas that might be marketable. Floyd Schlau's rolling dark blue Chevy story had circulated widely, and Howard set out to make the wheels roll with as little friction as possible.

He knew it was impossible to fit ball bearings into the small wheels, so he researched low-friction synthetic materials and found that a black plastic within the acetal family, a DuPont product called Delrin, provided high strength and stiffness with great dimensional stability and easy machining. Its inherently low coefficient of friction, the lowest of the affordable industrial plastics, encouraged him. Bearings had to endure radial loads,

those of the wheel on the ground holding the car up against gravity in this instance, and axial loads, those encountered in cornering as the centrifugal forces moved the car outward and the curb of the track held the car in. With some of Jack Malek's 0.008-inch diameter mandolin wire, Newman knew he was as close to zero friction as he could affordably get.

Newman's first versions, like those of Fred Adickes, used straight axles. He watched the kids in Rosemary Kazlow and Rita Rao's test rooms. He saw children put their fingers on the top of the car and push it down and feel the springiness. They got what he called a kind of "aha!" reaction. As he watched these children push the cars over bumps, the cars didn't exhibit the same spring reaction that real automobiles had. Even though the kids liked

46

these new cars very much and often refused to let them go at the end of play sessions, Newman set out to redesign the axle assembly. He devised new axles that looped between the wheels and stretched back from the front, and forward from the rear toward the center point of the car. He had created a miniature torsion-bar system for each of the four corners to provide the kind of full independent suspension only found in expensive sports cars at that time.

Fred Adickes' garage door weather seal prompted more serious track proposals, and within days, Elliot told any one who would listen that these cars needed to look fast and they had to prove their speed. Loops, jumps, curves, any stunt a real car could do on a thrill circuit Elliot wanted to see these new little cars do as well.

Marketing suddenly relaxed. There was clear and certain play value. Harry Bradley's designs looked like custom Camaros and Mustangs. And Howard Newman's suspension meant they had something they could patent, something of Mattel's own.

4

IDEAS HERE, PRODUCTION THERE,
BUT TAKE A LAWYER WHEN YOU GO BY AIR

According to Hot Wheels historian Mike Strauss, this car in metallic purple may be "the most remembered car of the era." This dream car made it into Hot Wheels production as the Silhouette in 1968.

Complete with play value, a new and exciting design direction, and a name to match, things accelerated with the velocity of a Hot Wheels car shooting down a track. Marvin Barab's packaging department was alerted. The cars needed a logo and a package that was as exciting as the product. Seymour Adler, senior vice-president of operations, and Vic Rado, vice-president of manufacturing, were notified to prepare for production numbers unlike anything Mattel had done before. Elliot and Ruth already manufactured Barbie dolls and other toys offshore in far-flung locations like Hong Kong, and they authorized the creation of die-cast tooling for the car bodies and plastic injection molds for the chassis. Adler and Rado needed to know how many cars would be made.

Product planner Len Mayem was deputized to sit in on a planning meeting in the middle of 1967 when his boss, Walt Ross, was out of town. It was a high-level gathering, populated with corporate executives such as Adler; Seymour Rosenberg, Mattel's new vice-president for finance; Bernie Loomis, the company's highest ranking sales executive; Frank Sesto, the head of manufacturing; Elliot and Ruth Handler; and a few others. One purpose of the meeting was to examine the question of whether or not to take Hot Wheels cars into production.

"Our sales forecast was for five million cars," Mayem said. "That represented a ten percent market share, which we felt was a reasonable number of the introductory year of the product."

Rosenberg, who had come out of the aerospace industry, still believed this was a sure way for Mattel to lose money. He looked at preliminary financial proposals and forecasts, which showed a huge financial loss on Hot Wheels development and sales. "Why are we showing a loss?" he wanted to know.

The group had to figure out how many Hot Wheels cars they could sell, and they also had to consider how many had to be sold in order to break even.

"This was a rather complicated calculation," Mayem remembered, "so I was excused from the meeting and I went into Elliot's office. This was before calculators and I started pushing my slide rule until it was smoking, trying to figure this thing out. There were so many factors, additional tooling, lead times involved, additional advertising, production, warehousing. I didn't even bother to consider how we were going to produce five million little cars. That wasn't my job to worry about. It was incredibly complex and so I made up a number. I went back into the room and told them, fifteen million cars, based on a number of assumptions."

Elliot looked at Seymour Adler. Could they make fifteen million cars? "They left the room and smoked their slide rules and when they came back, they said, yes, they could. Well, they didn't know any better if they could make fifteen million cars than I knew that fifteen million would break us even. It was a guess, a big guess. And they had no idea how to make the first one, let alone the rest of them."

Nobody had considered that fifteen million cars needed sixty million little wheels and each one would have a red circle stamped on it. A machine would have to imprint sixty million circles on a piece of plastic half the size of a dime. There wasn't any machine in the world that could to that job!

This miniature-car project, which had moved at a slow and almost secretive pace within Mattel for six or seven months, suddenly was about to be the "new toy." It had an astonishing number written into the production quotas column on Ruth Handler's TLP, the toy line projection spreadsheet. Mattel's engineering staffs counted experienced professionals with backgrounds in aerospace, automotive engineering, light and heavy

Mattel's designers for Hot Wheels cars come from a variety of disciplines. Designer Larry Wood dismisses his art skills, calling himself a car designer. His skill is evident, however, in these renderings of the classic Duesenberg SJ Dual Cowl Phaeton, released as the Hot Wheels '31 Doozie in 1977.

Within a few years after the Hot Wheels line was launched, Mattel encouraged children to fabricate their own cars. The Hot Wheels Factory kit provided everything a carmaker could need, including a press to seal the chassis, axles and wheels, interior, windows and body together tightly.

The candy colors of the early Hot Wheels cars set them apart from everything else out there. The attraction is easy to see from this colorful array of Custom Mustang variations. The 15 cars here, from Curtis Paul's collection, represent 14 different colors and variations such as open hoods and louvered rear windows. Several of the cars shown here are rare and valuable.

The Custom Barracuda, introduced in the Hot Wheels lineup of 1968, was based on the 1967 Plymouth muscle car. It is shown here in metallic light blue.

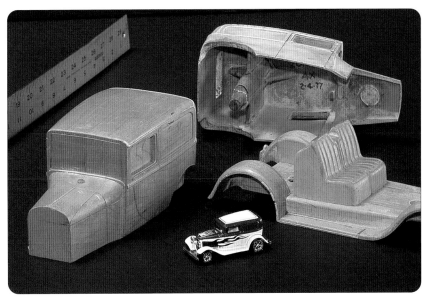

Model maker Steve Pennington carved this four-times-scale block model (left) and shell models (right and rear) of the A-OK in April 1977. Mattel held onto wood models such as these only for a limited period of time, but some were saved. They are part of a permanent display in the Hot Wheels Design Center.

equipment manufacturing, tooling design, and packaging among its members. These people had done these tasks countless times before. These were just initial concerns to address, just as legal and marketing had done. As designer Harry Bradley explained, "All Mattel's toys were extraordinary in their quality and their authenticity and their technology, and that's because Mattel hired the very best people." Those people asked questions and they did their homework.

"The idea of a free-spinning wheel on an axle was really essential to this whole project," Bradley said. "That little axle was bent like a hairpin, and suddenly there was flexion. It was almost like a

moment in history. I remember the moment when the first little mock-up was done and you could put your finger on that prototype and it would settle down and lift back up."

"Then someone handmade a little mag wheel and they got somebody to hand paint a Redline tire and it was another moment, Bradley recalled. "People were floating up to the ceiling."

To brighten up the cars, they repainted some prototypes with candy colors. Engineering people kept saying, "This is a toy, it's got to stand up under kids' abuse. We can always put a red stripe on a black piece of plastic, but it will wear off! And that color! That color has so many toxins in it, if a kid puts that

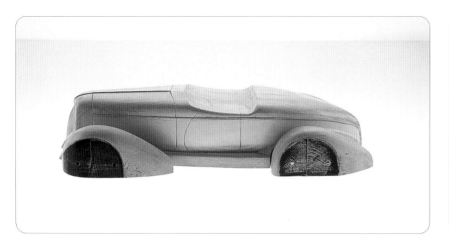

Wood block patterns of new car designs provided mold makers with the basic outside shape of the car or truck. This model for the 1934 Auburn 852, introduced by Mattel in 1979, was done by Industrial Design Affiliates (IDA) of Beverly Hills, California, an outside model-maker contracted by Mattel. Over nearly a decade, IDA did more than 100 models for Mattel.

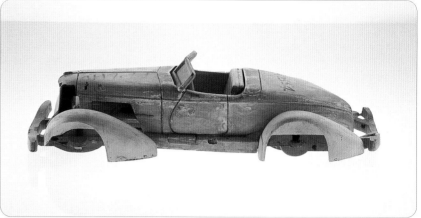

Once model makers completed the wood block pattern model, the next step was to produce a "shell" pattern, generally of epoxy, from which Mattel made the actual casting molds in 1/64th scale. The shell patterns, hollow inside, dictated to mold makers the forms that their casting molds must take.

in his mouth, he'll be laying on the floor four hours later with Xs for eyes and his tongue hanging out." Bradley laughed at this story thirty-six years after the fact, but they had used real candy colors for the first paint prototypes. Mattel, with its near-obsessive concern for child safety, would not even let those models out of the department.

Here is the disassembled Auburn 852 in shell molds. Missing are the grille and engine piece, which would fill in the radiator housing at the front and the engine compartment sides. In front of the car is the instrument panel and steering wheel, and the windshield piece is at the driver's door. This shell model is four-times the size of the production model.

Bradley explained how candy paint was applied on real hot rod cars: they first painted the entire car sliver, and then they put transparent color over it to give it the candy apple red or blue or whatever. Someone suggested zinc-plating the cars to give them a silver undercoat. A transparent non-toxic color over the plating would achieve the same look.

Elliot, Jack Ryan, and the marketing staff told Bradley to have at least one car each that represented GM, Ford, and Chrysler. He asked about American Motors, and the marketing staff sniffed and asked him to look in the parking lot and count the AMC cars he saw. There was only a handful. They told him they were not interested in anything that was not very famous or exciting to look at. It was a philosophy that kept AMC's Javelins and AMXs out of the toy line for the first few years.

Bradley was assigned to work with wood patterns and model-maker Jack Hargreaves. Hargreaves was known to have "golden hands." He came out of Detroit as a patternmaker for engine cylinders and cylinder heads for Ford Motor Company and body panel molds for General Motors. What made this relationship a challenge was that Hargreaves was in Hong Kong. He'd been there for a month or two already, trying to get another die-cast car operation going.

More than a year earlier, Mattel had purchased Hong Kong Industries (HKI) and its large seven-story factory complex in

Collectors love variations, small changes that designers, engineers, or production staff made in limited numbers. This metallic orange Custom Mustang has rare rear-window louvers.

This metallic gold fastback is much less common than other versions of the Custom Mustang. The open hood scoops allow the child playing with the car (or the collector viewing it today) to see the chrome engine under the hood. Mattel issued open hood scoop Mustangs only in red or this gold color.

Mattel engineers had the creativity and skills to give Hot Wheels cars added attractions like opening hoods and other movable parts. This metallic yellow Custom Mustang was released in 1968.

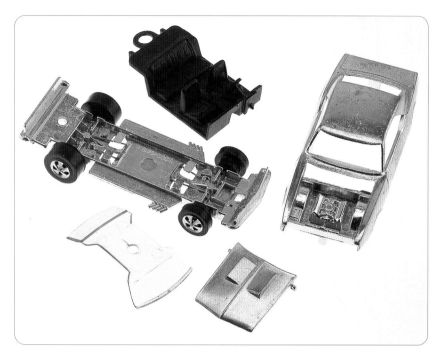

These are the parts that make up a Hot Wheels car: the zamac chassis, car body, and hood, and the plastic interior and window assemblies. Posts extending from the car body (visible at the front of the Custom Camaro shown here) extend through the interior and the window pieces to anchor them in place. A kind of drill press at the assembly station "spins" the posts, spreading the tips to secure the chassis and all interior pieces to the body.

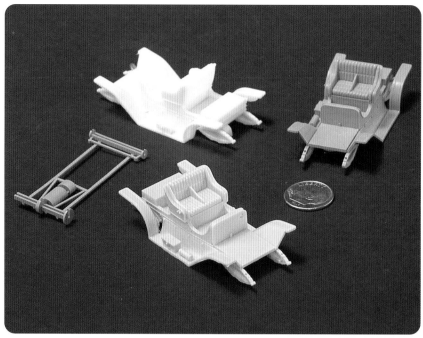

These are resin (the white or yellow-gold pieces) and epoxy (in brown) 1/64th-scale master mold models of the 1968 Hot Heap.

Kennedy Town on the east end of Hong Kong. The building was filled with several thousand women who sewed clothing for Barbie dolls. On a more thorough inspection of their purchase several months after the deal closed, Mattel staff found that the factory had a small die-cast operation working in a corner of one of the upper floors, complete with a small tool room. It produced die-cast cars for an outside client. Mattel shut the operation down immediately.

"Management was wondering what to do about this die-cast thing going on in Hong Kong," Hargreaves recalled. "There were about half a dozen old mechanically operated Battenfeld die-cast machines that opened and closed with a toggle-action clamp device. Either use them, or get rid of them, they thought. Newer machines are hydraulically operated, delivering much higher clamping pressures, necessary to handle high molten-metal injection pressures." Frank Sesto, director of manufacturing, visited HKI to evaluate if it ever could produce die-cast cars at the level of quality Mattel required. He concluded it was possible, but it would take

changes in everything from the attitudes of the employees to machinery and manufacturing operations.

"I got elected to go out there to get started on some small cars, ones a bit bigger than Matchbox," Hargreaves continued. "When I got there, the man who managed the building for us found some machinery locally and we set up a kind of model shop in the building. If you're starting out with blueprints when you set out to do a car, it's a long tedious route. For a short cut, I told the guys in Hawthorne, 'Let's just keep this lineup to things we can get a kit for, a plastic kit we can glue together.' All the popular cars were available in those days. So we bought a slew of 1/24th-scale kits and modified and changed them so I could lift epoxy molds off them so we could pantograph some cavities for die-casting."

A pantograph is a mechanical device used to reproduce a two- or three-dimensional object in the same, larger, or smaller scales. The device uses a framework of rods that appear generally like a parallelogram. Mattel's versions of these, and the kind other molding shops use, have a pin on one end that is used to trace the

This is a resin prototype of the A-OK, a Ford Model A two-door sedan delivery truck that Mattel introduced in 1978. Model maker Steve Pennington mounted this correct-scale-model prototype on Redline wheels, even though the Redlines went out of production in 1977. It was common for model makers and designers to scavenge parts from other models, their desks, or spare parts kits that they and their colleagues had assembled.

While the world knows this car as the Twin Mill, it had no official name when Ira Gilford completed the design. When young model maker Steve Pennington finished the prototype model on May 1, 1968, he carved the car's working name, Dream I, on the bottom. Meanwhile, in another part of the Mattel offices, Carol "Naming Lady" Robinson took one look at Gilford's two-engine concept and set in place another piece of Hot Wheels history with the name Twin Mill.

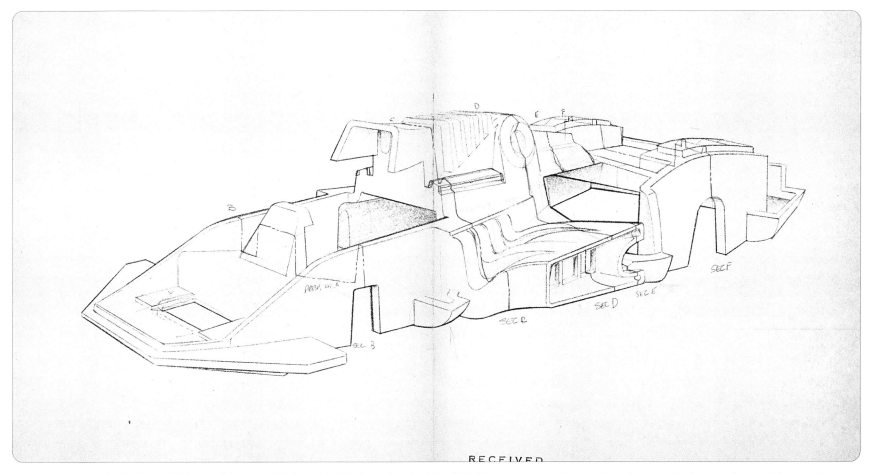

This blueprint drawing by Industrial Design Affiliates, dated April 1971, shows the short-lived Double-Header. Paul Tam and Larry Wood worked on the design of this model, which was introduced in 1973. Mattel kept it in production for this one year only. Red ink, or "red lines," on the drawing represents the section cut lines where IDA needed to do additional drawings and blueprints, and for modification IDA would have to make to produce a moldable casting.

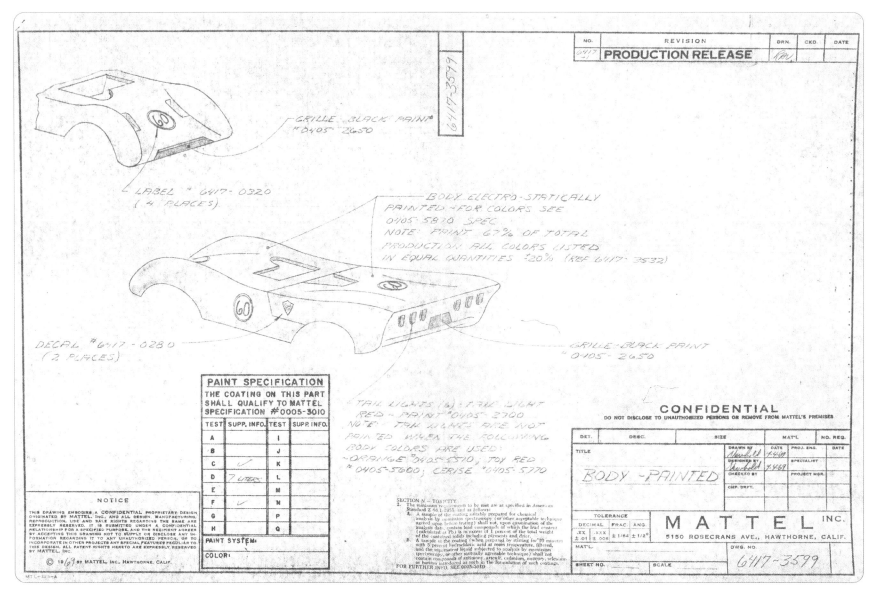

Once designers finished sketching proposed cars for the Hot Wheels line, engineering draftsmen created detailed blueprints for everything from the chassis plan to the decoration of the car. This is the paint plan for the Ferrari 312P, introduced as part of the Grand Prix series in 1970.

original. An extremely sharp rotating cutter on the other end carves the shapes that the pin transfers into steel blocks.

Hargreaves had to greatly simplify the kits, as Bradley had done. He eliminated the wipers, door handles, and all the other fine details that would not hold in the vast reduction. He also had to add draft to his molds, which allows the finished castings to come out of the machine. Hargreaves hired six men who, though not model makers, were good with their hands. His biggest problem was the language barrier. None of his workers understood a word of English, and his translators were fine for conversational needs, but words like "side slides," or "cores," or "undercuts" were beyond them.

"The interpreters really caused a lot of our problems. If they didn't know what you were saying, they would make a guess at it, a wild guess, or make something up. And most of the time they never admitted they were wrong. They weren't engineers and they didn't understand engineering. There were dreadful mistakes. We had a great amount of waste," Hargreaves said.

With this kind of die-casting, gates and runners direct the molten metal into the mold. Side slides are used inside the mold to block molten metal so the cast car would have side window openings and door seams. With the side slides moving in and out at the beginning and end of the process, Hargreaves had to figure out how to get the molten metal around the slides to

Mattel introduced the Ford J-Car in the first year of Hot Wheels cars, 1968. Though it was based on a Ford GT40 racing prototype that Carroll Shelby developed with Ford Advanced Vehicles in England, Ford completed work on the car at its design center in Dearborn, Michigan. There, young Ford designer (and future Hot Wheels designer) Larry Wood often went over during his lunch break to help designers and engineers from advanced design apply the tape racing stripes and other decoration to the full-sized version of the car.

where it needed to go. They did the molds and tried them out on the Battenfelds. The old mechanical presses were very slow and not suitable for fast mass production.

"We got the first two or three of them going, a Camaro and a Mustang, as I recall. I started out using the same axle that was on the old die-cast cars there, just a rigid axle about 0.050 inches, fifty-thousandths diameter steel, riveted over on the ends. We had no flexibility, no bendable axles, and no clearance around it either. It held proper scale from the sides," Hargreaves recalled. While this was going on in Hong Kong, things were evolving quite quickly back home.

"Plant One, back in Hawthorne, would telex me, saying what they were doing and what I should do. Someone back there had dreamed up the fine wire axles and little nylon wheels and Delrin bearings. That happened about midway through our project out in Hong Kong. So I started changing the epoxies and the models, opening up room for the wheels to move up into the car body, figuring how to mount these straight little wire axles. Then the next

morning we'd get another telex, 'No hold on, we're not going to do it that way, we had a meeting.'" Though he only spoke to them by phone about every third day, Jack heard from "Mahogany Row," as he referred to the executive offices, by telex regularly.

Hargreaves came in another morning to find a telex describing a new axle system and a new name for the toys. Until then, he and Hawthorne had just referred to them as the Chevrolet, the Ford. "By then, we'd made two or three of them, and we were well on the way." He went back to his drawing board.

The die-casting machines were dangerous. If they did not clamp tightly together, there might be a flash of metal left from an incomplete seal where molten metal had slipped out of the run and was sandwiched in another area. If a flash was not caught and removed, it built up to the extent that molten metal might squirt out in a spray between the gap.

"It didn't happen all that often," Hargreaves said, "but if it landed on your shoes, it would burn through the leather."

Hargreaves got the telex about the candy apple paint and its required zinc plating. He tumbled the cars in a rotating barrel plater. It was a more efficient method than dipping them into the zinc, and it created a lighter coating. Positively charged anodes are in the center of the tumbler, and the charge flows through the zinc solution from the negatively charged cathodes. As the cars tumble, they momentarily make contact with each other, the anode, and cathode. In that fraction of a second, the process flashes a little bit of zinc on the body. Early in the manufacturing process in Hong Kong, Hargreaves received a new Ransburg electrostatic paint system that took similar advantage of electric current, though it held the cars in electric contact for longer.

By charging the paint gun and grounding the paint racks where the lightly zinc-plated cars hung, the paint was attracted to the cars. As the cars rotated slowly inside the paint booth, much more of the paint ended up on the cars instead of being sucked up the exhaust fan.

"We hung the cars on a moving rack device, and they slowly went through the Ransburg in a circle," Hargreaves explained. "One end you load them, they'd revolve past the spray guns, and

For Hot Wheels engineers such as Bob Rosas, experimentation was always one of the assignments: develop new versions or appearances for existing models. At left is the more-or-less stock Custom Camaro, although it shows off oversized all-black wheels and an exaggerated raised back-end "hot-rod rake." In the center is an alternative paint scheme, done strictly to evaluate this combination for possible production. At right is a prototype Funny Car dragster that Rosas created using pieces he fabricated or scavenged from other models.

continue on into the infrared lights for drying, and ten minutes after you loaded them, someone at the other end was unloading the cars, fully painted. But we didn't use solid paint, it was a toner with some red, green, or blue in it. You could almost see through it."

By the time Hargreaves and his crew had three or four molds running, Mahogany Row decided the operation in Hong Kong could neither meet the quality standards nor match the quantity output that Mattel had set as targets.

"As I made the epoxies, the cores, and slides, I started shipping them back to California, and they jobbed them out to various shops around there. They cut the steel cavities, the molds, there. We'd already produced a few thousand of the cars, but we shut down the die-cast operation there and I came home.

"I'd made some interesting cars, but of course, all of Mahogany Row had heard that there was to be a new Corvette, and

they all decided we had to have it. There was no model yet, but you didn't say 'no' to Mahogany Row."

"**E**verybody there at Mattel wanted to do the Corvette," Harry Bradley recalled with a laugh. "They all understood it was going to be new, and so we also knew we couldn't do the old one, because that wouldn't be as exciting. I sketched the new car for them and they really went nuts."

The executives wanted to create a new model of the Corvette based on the new car's design, a radical evolution from the already radical 1963-1967 Sting Rays. Bradley had designed Cadillacs in his latter days at GM, and he had not worked on the Corvette project. He said he didn't know the proportions well enough to replicate the car. Security between design studios was very tight at GM, with locks on each studio's door. Founder Harley Earl, who had created the Corvette, and his successor Bill

Mitchell, who had adopted the car as his own, believed that cross-pollination of ideas, whether for Corvette design or Cadillac, diluted everyone's ideas. Designs, especially for a new Corvette, were covetously guarded.

Bill Mitchell had asked his designers to begin thinking about this new Corvette back in early 1963, even before Chevrolet's St. Louis factory started its preliminary assembly runs on the all-new 1963 Sting Ray. Chevy's product planners and GM management planned to keep the Sting Ray in production only through 1965 or 1966 at the latest, so it was never to early to start on the next car.

Mitchell set Larry Shinoda loose to create something dramatically new and, with influence from Zora Arkus-Duntov, Chevrolet's legendary engineer, one of the earliest versions was a wild mid-engined coupe that Chevrolet soon determined it would have to sell for at least $12,000. GM management knew that was much more expensive than any Corvette buyer would tolerate in those days. As design chief Bill Mitchell reined in the enthusiasm, he asked Shinoda to create a new personal car/show car for him to drive. Mitchell had enjoyed an earlier model, based on the 1961 cars, that he named the Shark. From Shinoda's emerging designs, Mitchell, an avid deep-sea fisherman, saw a new shape. He renamed his 1961 model the Mako Shark and then he took Shinoda's newest design and called it Mako Shark II. When viewers at the New York International Auto Show saw the wild concept vehicle in April 1965, they hoped they were seeing what the next generation Corvette might be. They had no idea how close it really was.

Following auto show raves, Mitchell shifted final design responsibilities to his other protégé, Hank Haga, in GM's California design studio (barely 50 miles from Mattel's own facilities). By November 1965, Haga's crew had completed full-size clay models. But production design work that Chevrolet management knew was necessary to complete the 1967 Camaro to

compete against Ford's Mustang held up the new Corvette. That setback gave Chevrolet designers time to try to incorporate an open-roof treatment from a Porsche model introduced for 1967, the Targa. They concluded that without the rigidity of a steel body, the Targa-type roof would not work on the fiberglass Corvette. Chevy's designers and engineers adopted a T-roof treatment from outside designer Gordon Buerhig. When Mitchell, Haga, and Shinoda rolled all these features into one body, the finished package was visually startling.

Based on Harry Bradley's speculative work, Mattel managed an introduction of Hot Wheels "Custom Corvette" that arrived at nearly the same time as Chevrolet's striking new 1968 Corvette (Chevrolet dropped the name Sting Ray for that one year to emphasize the difference between 1967 and 1968). Years later, designers and engineers from both sides say that each car helped sales of the other, feeding the frenzy of a wild new car and a fantastic new toy.

Mattel executives were determined to produce a version of the soon-to-be-released new 1968 Corvette, and the Hot Wheels Custom Corvette was part of the 1968 release. The top car shows the wear and tear from years of use compared to a recently restored version.

5

A LOGO, THE BLISTER, AND THE PROPHET

The 1968 introduction of Hot Wheels cars included many of the most popular American cars on the road. The 1967 Ford Thunderbird was introduced as the Custom T-Bird in 1968.

Jack Ryan's Preliminary Design group presented the Hot Wheels cars to Product Planning so they could come up with some proposals for what they could do with these cars. Jerry Fyre had moved into Product Planning soon after starting at Mattel in 1962 with a degree in Business Administration and Marketing from the Ohio State University. "Part of what we did was to define holes in our product line that we needed to fill, or opportunities that were there, to give some guidance to the designers," Fyre recalled. "We were called Product Planners, but really we were what today they'd call Brand Managers. If we do this, how do we give it play value and how do we develop it and expand it into something that will continue to be interesting?"

After Ryan brought the cars to Product Planning, Elliot Handler came into Fyre's cubicle. "You know, Jerry," he said, "those Hot Wheels cars we saw up there? We've got to come up with something for these cars to do. A track? Maybe a flexible track? With a clamp so you can attach it to a table or a chair to start the cars going?" Fyre remembered that Elliot made some drawings on a pad on his desk.

"'Go on up and show this to the design guys,' Elliot told me, 'and see if they can come up with something like that,' and he left and I flew out of my chair and went to see the guys who were just starting to work on Hot Wheels design."

At the next product meeting, Dennis Bosley and Derek Gable came up with a white extruded track and a c-clamp. They

The first car through the gates tripped the checkered flag, officially winning the race. As racing sets became more complicated, Derek Gable devised a finish-line sensor that clearly gave the victory to the first car to trigger the resettable flag.

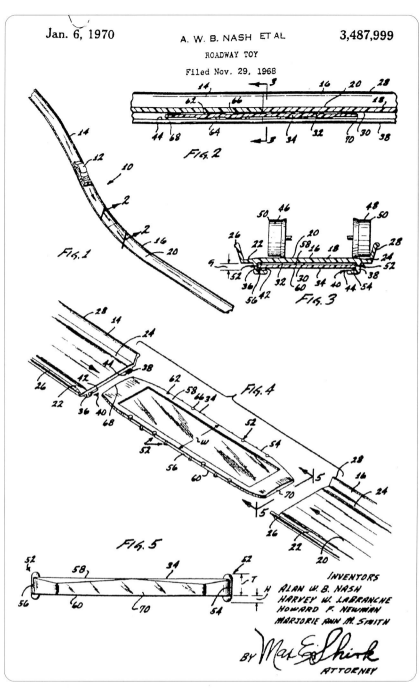

The patent calls this a "Roadway Toy," but the purpose of this patent was to protect Alan Nash's idea for joining one Hot Wheels track to the next. "The entertainment provided by scale-model automobiles," Nash wrote in his patent application, "can be enhanced by providing a toy roadway for guiding the vehicles along a smooth, swift path." Nash's creation, the tongue-like flexible plastic connector, fit into grooves manufactured into the track's base below the toy roadway. The flexible connector permitted loops or curves to fit neatly against rising or falling track sections.

attached two of them to the table, rolled out the track, and let two cars go in a race.

"And we all said, 'Gee, yeah, look at those little sons of bitches go. They can really go, can't they?" Fyre said.

Now that there was a track, Product Planning had to go back to work and come up with a line that would consist of individually packaged cars. A logo, designs, and labels needed to be created, and they still had to perfect the track. Fyre began planning sets (a car with several pieces of track) and accessory track sets so children could make the raceway as long as they wanted. The first white track was extruded, and the edges would curl outward and the cars fell off. They could never get the track to flatten out. Rolling it inward bent the edges in too much and pinched the cars, but it gave them the idea for loops that also had unexpected consequences. The cars were too low, their noses scraped at the beginning, and their tails lifted the cars off the track before the end of the loop. The prototypes went back to Jack Hargreaves for yet another revision. He raised departure angles, which are the angles between the ground and the front or rear of the car measured at the point where the wheel touches

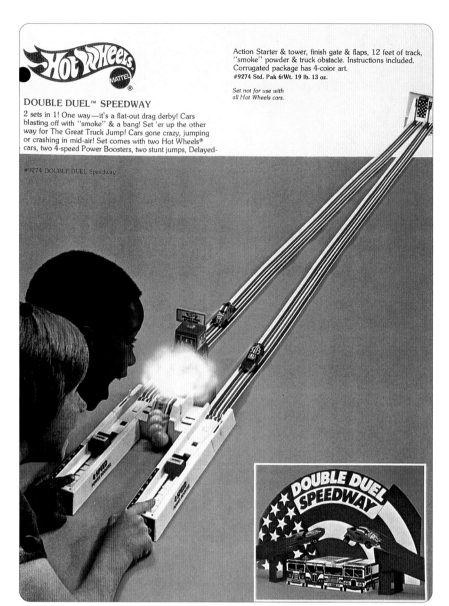

No sooner had Mattel patented its track features than it got them into production on racing sets. In the Double Duel Speedway, the starting gate released two cars at once and they raced down the drag strip to the finish line.

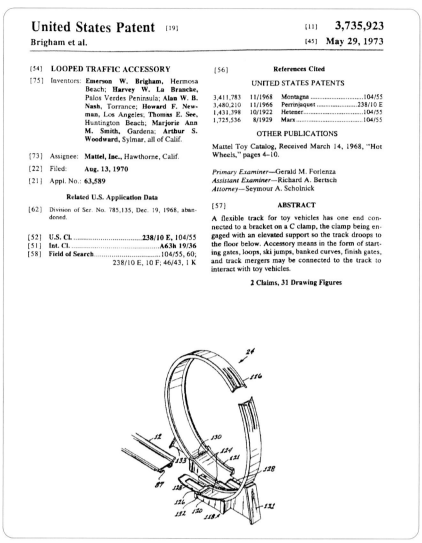

Mattel sought to patent its Hot Wheels loop in conjunction with a number of other track features, including a starting gate that children could clamp to a table top, banked turns, a jump, and a merging track where two cars slipped into a single lane. A prestigious crew of Mattel engineers participated in this collection. With the loop, they provided a novel and entertaining accessory for the track system.The Hot Wheels loop has been offered nearly every year since receiving the patent in May 1973.

the track. After that was adjusted, centrifugal force began to throw the cars off the loops because the little mandolin wire torsion bar suspensions couldn't handle the load. Engineers like Bill Summerfield raised ride height slightly by inducing a slight arc in the ends of the axles. Hargreaves opened up more wheel travel. More and more designers and engineers were drawn in from an ever-widening array of disciplines.

"The budget was very tight," Rick Irons said. "They were down to watching hundredths of a cent in designing the packaging and doing the cost. I was given a very strict budget."

Irons worked as a graphic designer in packaging design, alongside Ralph Parris who had been assigned to conceive the new toy's package, a varnished piece of cardboard about four by six inches with a clear display that showed the car. This is known as a clear blister and it marked another significant difference between the Hot Wheels cars a child could see inside the package and the Matchbox car inside the small opaque box.

"A little rectangular card at the point of sale wasn't going to make much of an impact, but as a designer, I wondered if we could give it some kind of die cut to make it look better than a rectangle, which was what most blister cards were at that point.

This play set from 1977 put two Hot Wheels cars through the dual "Corkscrew Super Looper" to race to the automatic finish line. Mattel introduced both the loop and the finish line components years earlier, but it refreshed their appearance and revitalized the track accessories each year as new enthusiasts grew up to play with Hot Wheels cars. This set was called the Thrill Driver's Corkscrew.

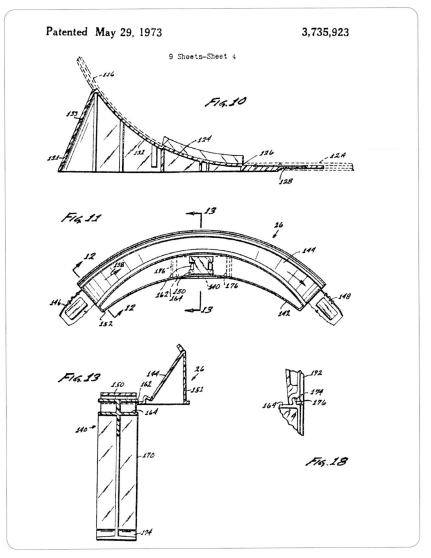

The high-speed banked turns (shown in the middle of this drawing) were another element of the blanket umbrella that protected the Hot Wheels loop as part of the "Looped Traffic Accessory" patent awarded in May 1973. The speeds that Hot Wheels cars reached made banked tracks necessary in order not to lose the car off the side of the track. Engineers Alan Nash and Howard Newman determined that Hot Wheels cars reached more than 200 scale miles-per-hour. That is the speed of full-size Indianapolis racers, yet those cars have much wider turns than Hot Wheels cars go through.

"I tried angles and zigzags, and finally, I settled on a horizontal S curve. Because the first working name they gave me was 'California Customs,' I just started working the curves and designing the logo to conform to that, to fit those letters. I thought about the flaming on cars that had been very big in the 1950s and 1960s, even back into the 1940s, so I started fooling around with a flame or a lot of them. I worked the lettering into the shape, but I was struggling a great deal trying to get it to read, to be readable. Then I heard it was Hot Wheels and everything just fit!"

Irons rapidly created all the Hot Wheels logos and labeling, and he designed the packaging for all the cars and for three new play sets that included pieces of track. He hired Otto Kuhni, an outside illustrator who was known for his artwork of airplanes and automobiles. Kuhni quickly created package illustrations of each of the models. As this happened, Ralph Parris struggled with the next challenge from Elliot Handler, a blister card package that could stand on its own.

"Elliot took a great personal interest in Hot Wheels," Parris remembered. "He felt very strongly that this was a winner, and he wanted to have a blister card that would either hang or stand. Up until that point, nobody had made a blister card that would stand by itself."

Parris, an industrial engineering graduate from the University of Michigan, had joined Mattel in 1962. While the cosmetics industry had used clear blister packs for a long time, this was a new idea.

"Elliot knew you limit where a store can put you if you have to hang your products on pegs, and he didn't want to be limited. Worse if they fell off the peg, they laid down. He wanted stores to be able to set them on a shelf or hang them." It was a novel solution to Marketing's challenge of no new shelf space.

"We had done a lot already with vacuforming other things. What I figured out was that normally when you form a blister, the platen, the base that you attach the tools to, is horizontal and flat. I put the platen on an angle so that when we pulled out the blister vertically, and took the blister off that platen, it would be, in effect, undercut, or like an overhang if you laid the package on its back. We had good modelers who could do things with their vacuform machines, and it worked fine in the model shop," said Parris.

The early development stages of Hot Wheels track led to innovative, exciting future products like the Criss Cross Crash Set. Power Charger boosters kept cars going at high speeds through turns and crossroads. Inevitably, one car met another at the intersection for a spectacular crash.

Nightmare Alley, another development from early track work, featured over-and-under banked turns and an intersection that required one racer to jump over the other. Miss the timing and the two cars crashed. The big-banked Terror Turn and other bends, twists, and jumps all included glow-in-the-dark decals for racers to stick onto the track.

This prototype of a Formula One racer was created by Derek Gable. Model makers completed assembly of this hand-made model in order for it to appear in sales catalogs, but Mattel decided against production based on the need to fit pods to other Grand Prix series open-wheel racers.

GRAND PRIX RACERS: TO POD OR NOT TO POD

Speed has always been a primary focus for the designers and builders of Hot Wheels cars. Since the beginning, Mattel's miniature vehicles have outpaced the competition on the miniature track. To further reflect the need for speed, many of the fastest real-life racers on the circuit have been produced in Hot Wheels form. In 1969, Mattel launched the Grand Prix series, featuring the most famous Can-Am, Indy, Formula One, and endurance racers of the era—all with a special touch of Hot Wheels style. The first year of Grand Prix cars in-cluded Jim Hall's Chaparral 2G and Bruce McLaren's McLaren M6A from the Can-Am series; the Ford Mark IV and Lola GT70 endurance sports-car racers; the Indy-style Lotus Turbine, Indy Eagle, and Shelby Turbine; and the John Cooper–designed Brabham-Repco F1, raced by Jack Brabham.

The extremely low center of gravity on the 1/64th-scale cars was true to the qualities of the full-sized race cars, and ensured excellent handling and the ability to negotiate tight turns and loops on the Hot Wheels track. The outboard wheels and narrow cigar-shaped bodies of the open-wheel racers, how-ever, would not work with the Hot Wheels Super-Charger accelerator. While designers experimented with adding plastic pods between the wheels on both sides of the cars, Elliot Handler raised the question of whether all Hot Wheels cars had to perform with all Hot Wheels accessories. In the end, matters of cost and child safety doomed the side pods. Because the pods were removable, creating a potential choking hazard, Mattel feared that children might swallow the small pieces.

The 1969 Grand Prix lineup included this Indy Eagle.

The Brabham-Repco F1 car remained in production from 1969 to 1971 and then reappeared in 1974 as a model called the Rash I. This chrome finish is very rare. The car's outboard Redline tires and wheels provided a minimum-friction surface to ensure faster running.

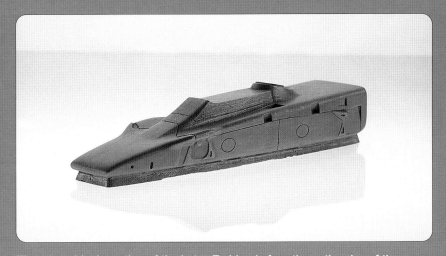

The epoxy block casting of the Lotus Turbine is four times the size of the production die-cast model.

Shown here in metallic red, the Lotus Turbine was put into production for 1969. An early production variation with a white plastic interior is considered highly valuable by collectors. The more common version has a black interior.

The real-life Shelby Turbine was raced by the legendary Mario Andretti. The Hot Wheels car is shown here in metallic blue with a chrome metal chassis.

Designers added side pods to the open-wheel Grand Prix racers to allow them to work with the Supercharger accelerator. Here, gray epoxy prototype pods fill in the sides of the metallic red Shelby Turbine.

Here the Shelby Turbine (light blue), Lotus Turbine (red), and Indy Eagle (dark blue) sport prototype pods. Risks outweighed the benefits, and Mattel dropped the last of its open wheelers in the mid-1970s. They returned when full-size racing technology saw engineering and aerodynamic benefits to their own side pods.

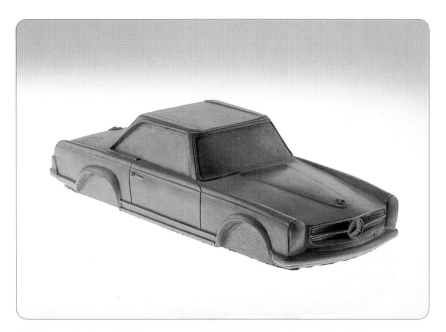

The Mercedes-Benz 280SL was one of the first Hot Wheels models of a European sports car. This gray epoxy master mold is four-times scale.

The Mercedes-Benz 280SL, introduced in 1969, is commonly found in metallic aqua, brown, green, or orange. This metallic gold is much less common and therefore is more highly valued by collectors, who prize rarity as well as undamaged condition.

That was just one blister, and if Elliot was right, Parris needed to be able to produce about fifteen million the first year. The process is different if you have to make that many. The blisters had to be made in numbers of about twenty per shot.

Parris and Bill Robb, a tooling engineer, figured a way to make a saw-toothed platen and alternated rows, one row uphill, the next downhill, or the reversed direction. It was a new vacuforming technique in order to get the blister to form that way. It was one of dozens of manufacturing problems, considerations, and techniques that had to be resolved over the next sixteen weeks Elliot had set aside for production startup.

Back along Mahogany Row, the debates continued. With Toy Fair less than five months away, Ryan's Preliminary Design department already had handed off many of the Hot Wheels concepts to the production engineers. Elliot had committed a budget for development, and Hot Wheels cars had a place on Ruth Handler's Toy Line Projection. The TLP listed every significant fact and figure for the toys already in or soon approaching production. It was Ruth's invention and it allowed her and the financial people to watch the money by watching schedules and sales. Behind closed doors, Ruth still wondered about the viability of Hot Wheels cars, but most people on the Product Committee, where the daily updates to the TLP were studied, confessed they had few points of reference for a product selling for less than a dollar when most of Mattel's toys cost multiples of that just to manufacture. It was generally acknowledged that Ruth's confidence in the idea was equal to about half of Elliot's enthusiasm. She pushed for production of five million cars, even at the risk of a slight loss, rather than seeing a larger write-off at Elliot's ten million car goal.

"The plan originally was to make around ten million little cars," Sam Djujic recalled. Djujic was Mattel's chief industrial engineer in charge of product costing, tooling, and plant design and layout. "This was as per Elliot's insistence and he finally allowed that if we couldn't get them out of the warehouse or if we couldn't sell any of them at all, that he personally would take responsibility for it," Djujic said.

Elliot dispatched his market research staff to the far corners of the country to test his hunch. One of the Mattel sales force who went along was Bernie Loomis, who had seen Mattel toys on the Mickey Mouse Club. In the late 1950s, he worked in New York as a toy manufacturer's representative. In that position, he had watched the birth of Barbie in 1959 and Mattel's talking doll

The '40s Ford 2-Door was first released in 1983 in black with a red, orange, and yellow flame, as shown in the blisterpack. It is shown here with a 1/6th-scale block model. The car was reissued in 1985 as the Fat Fendered '40, which is the version shown in turquoise in the foreground.

With Product Planning, Mattel could further the Hot Wheels cars brand and create NASCAR-themed cars. This hand-painted epoxy prototype shows the tampo decals for the NASCAR Stocker, released in 1983.

Because photographs for catalogs or advertisements only show one side of the car, the painter assigned to prepare this NASCAR Stocker for promotional materials needed only to decorate one side. Pre-production prototypes such as this one normally end up in the trash, but a few escape Mattel and end up in the hands of fortunate collectors.

The rapid growth of Hot Wheels cars led to a wide range of products that tied into the growing Hot Wheels phenomenon. The small plastic boy's wallet included a change holder inside.

Chatty Cathy in 1960. He met Ruth and Elliot at Toy Fair in 1961. They had mutual admiration and respect, and Loomis quickly accepted the Handlers' offer of a job in Sales.

"In the research process," Loomis explained, "we took a bunch of the best cars you could find, mostly Matchbox and I think there were some from Aurora at the time, and we put them in a box, just to get visual preferences. We had already developed a look that we called California Custom Styling. We took that box around the country. We asked the kids, 'Which one do you like?' Now this was visual only, we didn't use the name, there was nothing about performance, no chance to see how they performed, just how they looked. The result was just extraordinary. We had about twenty-four cars in the box, and the first eight choices each time were our new cars. We discovered we had something extraordinary in the styling even while those of us in marketing were all hepped up that we were going to have play value in the cars."

Mattel routinely would invite its top customers out for a private showing of its best hopes for the coming Toy Fair. While production engineers had cast solid brass prototypes of the first run of cars to check weights and balances to see if they could go around corners and do the loops without flying off the track, they also produced a few hand-painted prototypes meant for sales catalogs and for these private previews. These were done with painstaking care by two women in the doll face-painting department, Hiroe Okubo and Marlene Dantzer. Painting the prototypes, especially adding text like "Police Department" or a Ferrari logo, could take two full workdays. They used fine, triple-ought sable brushes to gently finesse the Cartoon Colors, the acrylic paints cartoon animators used. Once they were finished, the cars were sprayed with a coat of polymer gloss and off they went.

Kmart, which had grown out of Detroit's S.S. Kresge Company, was four years old at the time. It had opened its first 18 stores in 1962. By 1966, they had 162 stores, and Kresge reported sales of more than $1 billion. Sears was second largest, J.C. Penney was third, and a host of others, long since out of business, filtered down from there. Toys 'R' Us, founded in 1966, had just half a dozen outlets by this time. Bernie Loomis, Mattel's vice-president of Sales, invited Kmart's Ken Sanger, its boys' toy buyer, out for a sneak preview solely of the Hot Wheels line. Loomis hoped Mattel's best customer might give them an indication of the potential for Hot Wheels cars, along with a big order.

At this time, Mattel split into four divisions. With the reorganization, Mattel's board of directors officially named Ruth president of the company. Bernie Loomis, the head of the boys' division, was frustrated with Ruth because she wouldn't approve a production number large enough to justify production.

"We had mocked up some models in the second floor conference room for the show for Ken. I had a whole presentation prepared, and I had two strips of track laid down from a raised platform that ran down onto the floor. I started by holding up a Matchbox car.

"'Ken, you've been telling me how important this is.' I let it go and it ran down the track a little ways and fell off and somebody marked where it came off. Then I started to talk a little bit about the styling and I stopped and just said, 'This is something new. We call them Hot Wheels.'"

He let the car go down the track. It went way past the Matchbox car, off the end of the track, and along the floor. "I had a whole bunch of stuff I was going to say, but I saw a look on Ken's face. So instead, I just asked, 'What do you think, Ken?'"

"I'm going to hate myself for what I tell you," Sanger replied. "Keep it short at fifty million.'"

Loomis remembered the reactions among the Mattel brass. "Ruth and Elliot, and Cliff Jacobson, our V. P. of marketing, and my boss Herb Holland were all sitting behind him and their mouths slipped open. The first reaction we had from any buyer was that he would probably regret his decision to be conservative in his initial order of fifty million cars." After a single demonstration that lasted just a few seconds, Sanger either envisioned a doubling in the size of the die-cast car marketplace, or he had predicted the end of Matchbox.

When Sanger walked out of the conference room, he bumped into Len Mayem. He asked Sanger what he thought about the Hot Wheels cars. "He was so excited. His first words were, 'You'll sell every one you can make,'" Mayem said.

More than three decades later, Mayem observed that buyers have said that before and the product never sold. Most buyers are historians and not prophets. Very few buyers have the ability to be a prophet, and Mayem considers that Sanger was one of the few.

"I don't know where the shelf space came from. Ken Sanger, when he said he'd take fifty million, he didn't care where he was going to put them. They worry about shelf space when they don't see anything exciting. When they see a hot item, they'll make space."

6

AMASSING PRODUCTION,
CONFIRMING A NAME, AND TAKING THE PULSE OF SURFBOARDS

Ira Gilford designed this concept car, introduced in 1969 as the Splittin' Image. This black-painted prototype was from an early pre-production run to test the Ransburg electrostatic-paint spray guns in the paint booths. Black paint cost much less than the Spectraflame colors, and when black dried, it showed casting flaws more clearly. Black-painted cars often went all the way through the assembly process to ensure the proper fit of all the parts.

Mattel's original plan was to manufacture Elliot's ten million cars at Hong Kong Industries (HKI). When the first previews went so well, the company recognized that they could sell more than just ten million Hot Wheels cars. Mattel assigned the bulk of assembly to HKI, but it also would produce some of the cars domestically.

Sam Djujic, Mattel's chief industrial designer in 1967, had learned that at Mattel, industrial design was applied in a classic way with product cost, tool development, and plant design and layout.

"My task, even if it took an army of people, was to get Hot Wheels cars off the ground, get them into production, and get production up to a million cars a week, as quickly as possible, even if it meant assembling them

and packing them out by hand. They talked me into accepting the responsibility. There was no automatic tooling initially. We were going to assemble them in-house, but they were going to be die cast in an outside facility, A&A Die Casting Company, and the plastic parts, the interiors, and window glass were going to be molded at H&H. That's what brought about Mattel's purchase of H&H Injection Molding Company, and then of A&A. Hot Wheels cars made management at Mattel recognize that now we had a base where we could use the total, entire capacity of these two kinds of operations.

"Everybody looked at this little car that had a die-cast body and chassis, an injection-molded interior, and these four little wheels and axles. From a manufacturing standpoint, there was no challenge here, everybody said. It was a no-brainer. Just push the button and they should start coming down the conveyor."

But there wasn't a conveyor or a button to push yet. Even after Jack Hargreaves shipped the die-cast molds back to California, R&D dithered with the formula and finally settled on zamac, a zinc-aluminum alloy, because it gave the cars the weight needed to take advantage of a gravity start.

Toy Fair opened on February 15, the same day that Chuck Williams, Mattel's vice-president of quality and safety, and Seymour Adler, vice-president of operations, met with Sam Djujic, Frank Sesto, newly named head of manufacturing for Hot Wheels, and Gene Barker, recently hired to manage quality control, reliability, and safety for Hot Wheels. Williams and Adler took the men out to the 200,000-square-foot warehouse behind the main building in Hawthorne, which was adjacent to the 405 freeway at Rosecrans Avenue. Williams showed them a Hot Wheels prototype toy.

"Their idea," Barker explained, "was that on any given model, we would only do a limited production run, perhaps three months, to prove the tooling, and then they would shut the line down and transfer production to Hong Kong. Our plant at Hong Kong Industries would manufacture the cars, send them back to us, and we would do all the packaging, since that was the bulkiest part of the operation, the most costly to ship."

What happened instead was that once manufacturing turned a given car on, it never had the chance to shut it down. The demand was so great that once Barker's staff proved the tooling, they brought up duplicate tooling in Hong Kong. Meanwhile, they continued to run the original product for the rest of the year in Hawthorne.

According to Frank Sesto, the chief problem they encountered was that a lot of the equipment had to be designed from scratch. "Buying off-the-shelf components and assembling them for our specific use was one way to solve the problems. But we also had to staff the tooling groups and engineering groups.

"One fact that restricted production was that Mattel produced the cars in the U.S., and it used a totally different production concept at HKI. Mattel had used single-shot machines running at

This unpainted zamac prototype of the Classic Nomad illustrates several interesting developments of early Hot Wheels engineering. The blackwall tires with alternate plastic inner rims were a result of Mattel's efforts to save costs by eliminating the red lines from the tires. Engineers also experimented with a variety of plastics and compounds that might increase or at least maintain speed while decreasing manufacturing cost. Another chassis improvement is visible in the axle system. By the time Mattel introduced the Classic Nomad in 1970, the axle and suspension system was greatly revised and simplified. The now-straight axle, pinned in place by a spun-on plastic panel, anchored the axles accurately while still allowing the effects of a full suspension.

Another example of a rare black prototype, the Chaparral 2G was part of the 1969 Hot Wheels line. Most black cars were destroyed at the plant. Some workers were attracted to the unique, plain models and tossed them in their work boxes, discovering them months or years later. By then no one at Mattel cared about "old" cars.

The Porsche 911 was always a popular car among Mattel staffers, both in 1/64 and standard scale. Both the engineering and production departments made use of unpainted die-cast car bodies like this, each of them making certain other parts fit together well with this correctly proportioned sports car replica.

high speed, and it couldn't buy enough machines that would work fast enough to produce fifteen million cars a year."

Mattel also insisted on extremely high quality standards: casting quality, paint, decoration all had to be perfect. "What we were throwing away would have been a high quality product from another company. The scrap rate was horrendous," explained Sesto.

"Obviously," Barker said, "you needed a really smooth die cast because any imperfection of the die cast came through the paint. But you could have the greatest looking die cast, and if you didn't get a good paint job—well. So we were painting electrostatically, using the Ransburg system." Mattel also started looking for outside plants to outsource production, because before too long demand had reached 200,000 or 300,000 cars per week.

Mattel cast this orange resin body as the male correct-scale block model for the Hot Wheels P-911. From this, model makers formed the female mold forms to cast the entire car body. "Slides" are inserted through the mold during the molten-metal pour to allow for the open windows.

In late 1975, after introducing the regular production P-911 model in yellow and then in white, Mattel ran another 200 cars in gold chrome as gifts along with an explanatory plaque to its top sales staff.

"All our attempts to automate," Sam Djujic recalled, "with the exception of a couple of operations in wheel assembly and decorating, never materialized. With the exception of three or four operations, it was all manual labor. Obviously the electrostatic painting was done on an automatic conveyor, but the cars had to be racked and the racks hung on the conveyors to go through the painting and drying process, and then removed again by hand."

Assemblers loaded a chassis with the four z-shaped axles and wheels, and then secured the axles in place. They turned the body upside down and set it into a mask (a jig that cradled the body without scratching the paint) so they could insert the interior. The overturned chassis was set on the upside-down body and the body was "spun" onto the chassis to seal the rivet system.

"To spin the body onto the chassis," Djujic continued, "you have a little drill press, but instead of drilling into the car, the drill jaws held a concave bit, so as you came down with the spinning bit and you applied manual pressure, it started to heat and it deformed the zamac until it ultimately spread into something like a rivet head, sealing the chassis onto the body." This was all done manually. A huge crew worked in the factory as they struggled to reach production of a million Hot Wheels cars a week.

The metal badges that came with the early cars were developed in the marketing department. Hot Wheels logo creator Rick Irons designed the little round pieces with a tab to fold over a pocket or a belt. The idea was to promote child-to-child marketing, so that when they looked at each other's badges, they would wonder which car the badge came from.

"The worst challenge was the wheel and the axle," Sesto recalled. "I really believe it was over-engineered for what we were getting from it. That design was probably the toughest thing to produce. It had so many nuances that if anything went wrong in the system, the car would not perform. And performance was crucial. There were standards, and tests."

The Silhouette is nothing if not strikingly stylish. Mattel produced this and all its 1968 cars between plants in Hawthorne, California, and Hong Kong. Each plant did things slightly differently, using nearly but not perfectly duplicate molds. As a result, there are distinctions that are discernible to the most devoted collectors. The version shown here was produced in the United States.

Variations created for the Europe market are also appealing to collectors. Mattel introduced the Custom Volkswagen in 1968, with an exposed, supercharged front engine and a sunroof, as is the case with the metallic green model. The European version, in metallic blue, lacks a sunroof.

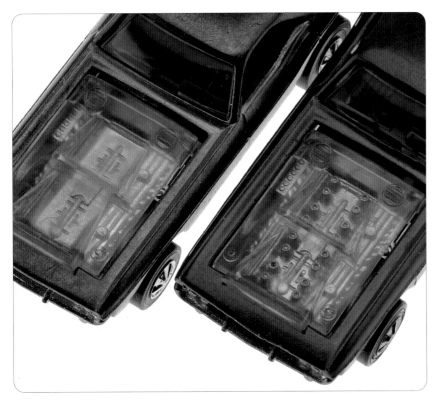

Collectors look for, and thrive on, car variations. Here are two versions of the 1971 Bye-Focal, Larry Wood's version of a tandem-engined Dodge Challenger funny car. Under the clear plastic hood, the metallic blue version shows fuel injector stacks, whereas the metallic green car has a much simpler plastic casting. Because the simplified version without injector stacks is the rarer of these two, it is more desirable and valuable.

In addition to the challenges of a tiny axle, the wheel bearings were made from Delrin, a special material that had the lowest coefficient of drag of anything out there. Local independent shops molded Delrin in small injection-molding machines and then inserted the tiny pieces inside the wheel or tire. Mattel helped many injection-molding companies begin business. When they needed more capacity, Mattel's purchasing department would call up one of their tooling vendors and suggest they get some machines because Mattel would keep them busy with Hot Wheels work.

Handling the bearings was difficult as well. "It was like dealing with rice kernels, having to work with something so small," Sesto recalled. "You could lose 100,000 of those things if you misplaced one small box.

Production started slowly. Djujic and Sesto hired workers, created work stations, and debugged Ransburg paint lines. Because the small cars gathered cost in raw materials as they progressed along the line, Sesto and Djujic cut assemblies

This was Larry Wood's first design for Mattel and the Hot Wheels line, done in September 1969. It was named the Tri Baby for its three engines, and was released in 1970.

short as they proved new tooling or line set-ups. Pilot production cars avoided the Ransburg machines and new hires learned to spin bodies, which saved the cost of paint on the cars that might be damaged in the learning process. However this yielded the occasional completely assembled raw zamac body. Setting up new Ransburg lines produced cars in black only as technicians adjusted guns and nozzles. Both of these procedures resulted in cars now highly valued by collectors. Mattel selected a custom blend of Glidden paints for the transparency to achieve the candy colors.

Personnel funneled dozens of new workers every day into the new plant. New hires were warned to expect unconventional days off to allow for seven-day workweeks. The advertising and marketing staffs also worked long weeks.

On Saturday mornings about once a month, the advertising research staff of marketing research leased out a commercial movie theater. Pete Folger ran the program for a while. They had a number of variations of the Schwerin test to determine product awareness, test the waters for a new product, or test the effectiveness of new commercials.

"In addition to running the regular children's feature, we'd run a pod of Mattel commercials before the feature began. This is a standard technique called the Schwerin Test, in which you take a pre-measurement of a person's attitude, introduce a stimulus, and then after a decent seasoning period, you test them again to see if the stimulus has altered their reaction."

An emcee asked the children in the audience, often as many as 400, to circle the toy they would like to win at the end of the day. They each had a prize pad with pages that showed four examples of several toy types on a page. On the car pages, one car was a Matchbox, one a Hot Wheels, and two from other manufacturers. Underneath each picture, it said the name of the car.

"We worked hard to match the pictures, all black and white on all the pages, and all four of the cars looking pretty much the same; four coupes, for example. The Master of Ceremonies on the stage moved the kids through the pads, and on the car page, he asked if they wanted a Matchbox or the Corgi or the so-and-so or the Hot Wheels. This was early on, before Hot Wheels cars were introduced, before anyone had even seen one."

Folger ran the commercials and the theater showed the movie. After the movie, the emcee asked the children to fill out the prize pads once again. Then Folger finished up the program, some kids won toys, the children went home, and Folger and his staff went back to work.

"Normally, if you show a page with four things, you'd think that roughly twenty-five percent of the audience would pick each of the four. Then you show your commercial and maybe the commercial would result in your twenty-five percent

The Turbofire was another Ira Gilford concept car created in 1968. Mattel introduced it in 1969. The pre-production prototype shown here features black paint used during the development process.

Elliot Handler approached Ira Gilford one day and proposed a series of concept trucks. Handler wanted the truck chassis to remain unchanged, but the box, tank, crane, or loader on the back could be interchangeable. Gilford created the Heavyweight series. The Fire Engine was one of the first six released in 1970.

As Gilford's Heavyweight Fire Engine neared production, Mattel product planners concluded it needed a ladder. Model makers fabricated a prototype ladder that appeared on this pre-production model as a white piece. In final production, the ladder came in black, and Mattel then added white hoses.

Designer Ira Gilford created the legendary Twin Mill concept not as a car with two engines but instead as a car with an exposed rear end featuring very fat tires. With so much space left in front of the passenger compartment, he drew in two engines almost as an afterthought. Prototypes appeared with two different rear fender configurations. Mattel went into production with the more abbreviated fender shown here on the metallic gold car.

IRA GILFORD

Harry Bradley, the "car guy" brought in from Detroit to help lead Mattel into the die-cast car world, left Mattel in the fall of 1967. He was told the company didn't think the cars were going to be particularly successful. Since he seemed resolutely to be a car designer and not a toy creator, Mattel felt it was not the right place for him.

Within months of Toy Fair and weeks after hundreds of children told Pete Folger they wanted a Hot Wheels car, Mattel called Bradley back. By then, however, he was dealing with the Japanese car companies. He was happy in his new position, but he recommended a friend of his at Chrysler, Ira Gilford.

Gilford worked at Chevrolet and had done a great deal of the work on the T-top roof system for the real 1968 Corvette. He had been promised a promotion, and when that didn't come through, he went to Chrysler. After a promised Studio Chief position failed to materialize there, he was ready to move on. Bradley called him, told him who to call, and within a day Gilford packed his family in a car and headed for California.

He arrived at Mattel in early 1968 and scarcely lifted his head from the drawing board. Gilford remained there for only eighteen months, but in that time he produced more than forty cars. The 1969 Hot Wheels lineup included such legendary Gilford designs as the Twin Mill, Splittin' Image, Torero, and Turbofire. His imprint on the 1970 introductions can be seen in the Swingin' Wing, the Power Pad, and the inaugural Heavyweights. The Heavyweights came out of an hour-long discussion with Elliot Handler about how a basic design might

work for a line of trucks. Elliot suggested he experiment with how various truck functions might work on a common chassis. The result was a futuristic series of work trucks and emergency vehicles for 1970 and 1971.

The Fuel Tanker joined Gilford's Heavyweights line in 1971. Regular production models appeared only in white enamel paint with a white plastic tank. This prototype was painted in purple for catalog photography and evaluation purposes. Two retractable black hoses emerge from the rear of the tank.

Harry Bradley, a native Southern Californian and lifelong hot rod enthusiast, rankled when Elliot Handler proposed adding two tiny plastic surfboards to his Dodge Deora show car.

choice going up to fifty percent, if you're lucky. That would be pretty good!

"The problem," Folger continued, "was we had something that had never happened to us before. We almost couldn't measure it. The pre-exposure measure, the first pads before the commercial, was up near eighty percent!" Folger laughed. "Now maybe, in that category we might have expected Matchbox to get fifty percent and the other three cars would have shared the other half, especially if one of the cars wasn't even available yet! Hot Wheels, just the name, did it."

The result of the test was about a ten-percent increase, from eighty to ninety percent. It didn't prove the overall effectiveness of the commercial, but it did prove the overwhelming appeal of the cars.

Harry Bradley wanted to incorporate show cars into the Hot Wheels line. He told Mattel about Ed "Big Daddy" Roth and his car, the *Beatnik Bandit*. Roth had signed a contract with Revell to license a model car, which Roth and Bradley feared might prevent Mattel from producing it as well. The owners of Revell and the Handlers were social acquaintances, however, and the matter was resolved over a friendly dinner.

Another famous show car that Bradley wanted to introduce in Hot Wheels form was the Dodge Deora, which he had designed for

Chrysler while working at General Motors. The car was built by Mike and Larry Alexander and was a very successful show car. AMT had created a model from it, and the people at Mattel loved the car.

"But the Deora suddenly became a no-no," Bradley recalled, "because there was no power-dome on the hood, and it couldn't open. And we wouldn't open the back because we were going to do that on the Custom Fleetside, which was a copy of my own El Camino."

Someone suggested putting surfboards on the Deora, an idea that horrified Bradley. "In those days, car guys hated surfers and surfers hated car guys. The two cultures were sort of galactically separated. They thought we were stupid people who messed up otherwise-good cars when we could be out surfing, and we just thought they were dumb. The idea of putting surfboards on my

Deora was absolutely unacceptable to me, and I damned near got myself fired over it.

"'We just can't do this,' I said. 'We can't put surfboards— Look, it's a guy's car, it's full of horsepower and style. Surfboards make it look silly.'"

Elliot replied, "We're putting surfboards on it, and that's it."

In retrospect, Bradley sees it was simply a great idea. "That proved to be a very inspired piece of problem-solving and marketing. It also was a good lesson for me, because I learned to get out of my little groove, my little car thing, and begin to think cross-culturally. That was the thing about Mattel. They could really see a bigger picture, Elliot especially. He had his fingers on the pulse of what made a good toy, and even more importantly, what was a good idea."

7

PRODUCTION FOR THE MASSES

The New York Toy Fair has always been the biggest opportunity for Mattel and other toy companies to show off new products to buyers for the coming holiday season. Mattel spent millions of dollars each year to create elaborate displays of boy's and girl's toys. Mattel also produced small "thank-you" gifts for buyers and customers who visit their displays during Toy Fair. In 1975, the Super Van became the first Hot Wheels car to get a special design treatment for Toy Fair. To make sure that the Toy Fair decoration fit on the new Super Van, model makers painted the logos by hand on a white plastic prototype *(left)* before going ahead with printing tampos onto the gold chrome commemorative edition *(right)*.

Back in the factory, Sam Djujic, Frank Sesto, and Gene Barker needed a fleet of trucks to haul the toys. They also needed an unending series of miracles to keep production going and come close to quotas. From the middle of February until Christmas Eve, these three worked every day in a plant that was close to twenty-four-hour work days. By late summer, nearly 3,000 workers assembled Hot Wheels cars. Djujic established 50 assembly lines and Barker hired almost 500 quality inspectors to randomly check tens of thousands of cars a day.

"Cars were produced in tiny lugs. A lug is a heavy cardboard box and ours were about ten inches by ten by twenty-two, each containing 256 cars," Barker explained. The assemblers were to review every car before they put them in the lug. Then inspectors pulled random samples from each lug. The amount of inspection on this product was far in excess of most of what Mattel did on any other product. The volume was higher than anything else Mattel ever had done.

The primary functional test inspectors ran on a regular basis was to send the car down the track off a two-foot high ramp. They made sure the cars ran at least fifty feet and recorded the actual distance. They continuously monitored distances so if there was a significant decrease, they would look into the process to locate the problem.

Barker and his senior staff established paint color deviation standards and quality standards for the stamped redlines. While they always sought a full 360-degree circle, they would accept a circle as low as 358, but would contact the supplier.

The small blister card was a challenge of almost gargantuan proportions. Manufacturing used a silicone product to release the clear blisters from the vacuform machines, but silicone caused the glue to be useless if the lubricant ended up where the blister stuck to the card. Ralph Parris hoped to use one blister size to fit all the cars, but they soon learned there was no way the Custom Fleetside would fit in the Custom Mustang blister.

Parris constantly investigated new techniques and new materials. He regularly called in different plastics companies. What they had to say sometimes surprised him.

"I remember DuPont sent their vacuform expert over and I was showing him the blister, just the single prototype we had made in the model shop, to see if we could do it. 'This is what we want to do,' I said. [He said] 'Yeah, well, that's impossible. You can make one in a model shop, but you can't do lots of them like that in production.'

Parris replied, "'Oh, well, do you want me to show you the machine we're going to try to do this on anyway?'

"We went down there, and it was running, beautifully, perfectly, cranking out something on the order of a hundred thousand every shift. He stood for a moment looking at the machine and said, 'Oh, well, sure, if you do it that way.'" Parris laughed hard at the memory. "That was one of my proudest moments."

Challenging those great moments were the badges. Parris needed to match the badge to the car, to the artwork on the package, to the blister, all at the rate of a 100,000 a week. Mattel increased production to 100,000 a day, and by December, it reached 1,000,000 a week. Harry Bradley's Deora with the surfboards caused the packaging staff and quality inspectors their own headaches. First the car required its own blister that held the boards onto the truck bed, but not so tightly so that in transport, the blister rubbed against the boards or the Deora to abrade the car or rub off any paint.

Blisters were shipped in master cartons and packed head-to-toe, back-to-back, and front-to-front, with 128 cars in a carton. Every day quality inspectors, part of a group known as Corporate

The California Custom hot rod had been a design and styling goal of Hot Wheels cars from the earliest days in 1966, but the Hi-Rakers Series introduced in 1980 took it in a new direction. These cars mimicked the hydraulic suspensions that became a trend among hot rodders and customizers in the late 1970s, particularly in East Los Angeles. Mattel produced the 3-Window '34, '40s Woodie, Dodge D-50 pickup, and Split Window '63 Corvette as Hi-Rakers. This prototype by Derek Gable was created from a gold-chrome 1974 Rodger Dodger.

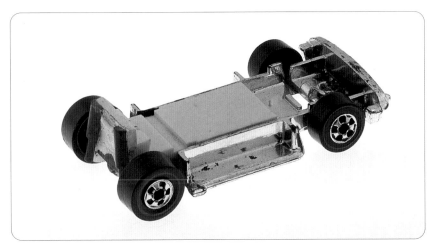

The rear portion of the Hi-Rakers chassis flipped up, or jacked up, to force the car's nose down in the traditional "hot rod rake."

Audit, randomly selected a pallet load of master cartons that had been completed and sealed during the previous twenty-four hours. They took these up to the Reliability Lab and tested them more extensively than the Quality Inspectors. First they shook a sealed carton on a vibrating bench for thirty to forty minutes, roughly equal in violence to a 100-mile truck ride. As soon as it came off the table, the inspectors dropped the box on any corner of their choosing from at least three feet. Then they opened the box and inspected the contents.

First they checked to see if what was inside was what the box labeling said it was. They looked for failed blisters, cars fallen to the bottom of the carton, or cars inside the blister that had turned around, flipped over, or had abrasions on their roofs or sides. They also looked at overruns of the glue from the blister that may have stuck to the car.

"The reality with Hot Wheels," Barker said, "was that we probably could have Scotch-taped them shut because nobody really cared since they were in such demand. And that was one of my constant challenges because there was always someone who felt we were too stringent for quality because the market would take any product that got out there."

By November, as they hurtled through production to meet Christmas orders, the warehouse had nearly 5,600 assemblers who worked three shifts every day. Barker's reliability and

Mattel's product planners threw their engineers another design challenge with the concept for "flip-out" cars. The cars featured a spring mechanism inside that would cause the car to flip over when it collided with a car in front. One version was designed to flip end-over-end, while another variation launched the car over on its side.

This prototype flip-out car was made from the Custom Continental. The large snow-plow front bumper triggered the oversized spring inside the car that kicked the car off the track. Releasing the spring throws the Continental quite a distance.

In the mid-1970s, Mattel engineering began experimenting with steerable Hot Wheels cars. This 1975 model Super Van has an early prototype front-steering system. As with the large Custom Continental, engineers preferred experimenting on the Super Van because its size gave them room to work.

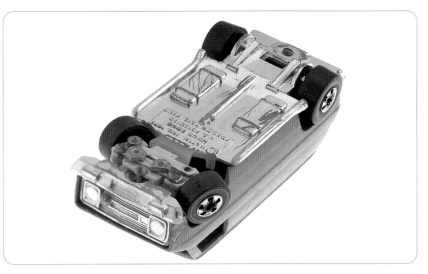

This view of the underside of the steering prototype Super Van shows Derek Gable's re-creation of automobile steering equipment reduced to 1/64th scale. The steerable cars never made it beyond the experimental stage because no one outside Mattel had asked for steerable Hot Wheels cars, and they were very expensive to mass produce.

quality standards never relaxed, but to further monitor things he and his staff turned to the phones.

"We would try to call a couple of people who had returned toy registration cards and talk to them about the product," he explained. He made some of the calls himself. "What did they like about it, what didn't they like? What other kinds of Mattel products did they have? And the thing I remember most was how astonished people were when we called them up asking how they liked a one-dollar toy. We fed that information on to marketing and engineering. It gave us the pulse of what people liked, and what they wanted. And that first year of course, the biggest question was where can I go to get more."

Sometimes, the people called back.

"After five in the evening, many of the phone lines that came into Mattel were redirected back into the manufacturing shops. Our phones would ring until late in the evening, [the

Another attempt at making steerable Hot Wheels cars resulted in this Mercedes-Benz C-111 with a small steering wheel on the dash. The slot cut into the windshield allowed the child to steer the C-111 left or right. Derek Gable used this black-paint test car because it was a handy "guinea pig" that he found in his desk drawer.

people] asking if they could just stop by and buy product directly from the loading dock. We got phone calls on Christmas Eve that first year. At four o'clock, we were finally trying to shut down for the holiday week. We were trying to get out of here, and people were calling in. They were lined up at the gate, trying to buy Hot Wheels cars. There was no product available any place." Short supplies led to problems inside the plant as well.

"We'd be production-piloting a new car down one of the start-up lines," Djujic said, "running these black cars and then even the first production-run models. We had a big problem with our own people taking cars. The top of the conveyor would be packed with parts starting down the line. I'd stand at the bottom and less than half was coming off in complete cars. Our security people had a hell of a time. People got really creative.

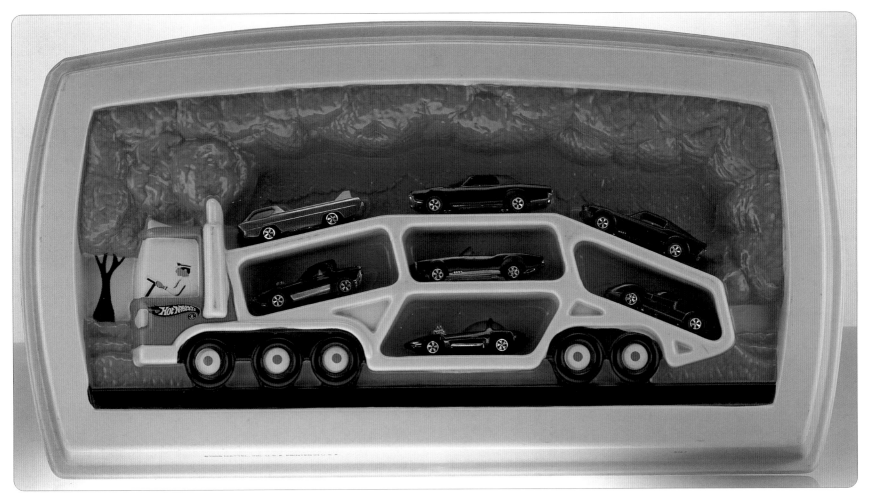

Mattel understood from the start that some of its buyers would want to display their Hot Wheels cars, just as Matchbox owners did. Mattel put style and humor into their late 1969 wall display unit, creating a stylized auto-transporter with room for seven Hot Wheels cars. Here the display contains a gold Deora, blue Rodger Dodger, red Mustang, pink Python, green Firebird, green Ford J-car, and purple Silhouette.

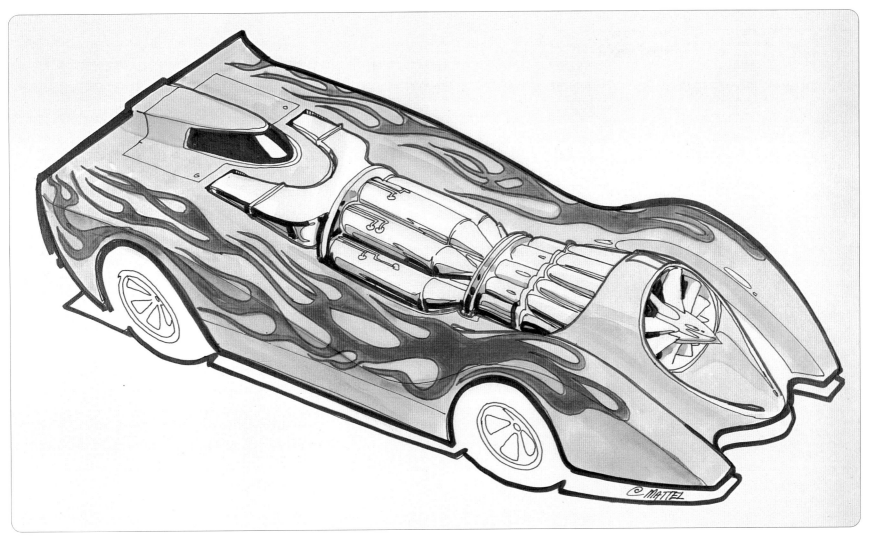

One of the most famous cars from the desk of designer Larry Wood was introduced in 1971 as the Jet Threat. This concept drawing from May 1, 1975, shows an updated design for Jet Threat II, which was introduced into production in 1976. A third version, the Jet Threat 3.0, took the car into the twenty-first century as part of the 2001 lineup.

"The maintenance people who serviced the Ransburg equipment or the drill presses used to come in with their Thermos bottles. At least two of them got caught at the gates. Their Thermos bottles were phony and they were loaded with the latest cars. The security people knew that if we piloted a car on a Thursday or Friday, they would go to the local swap meets on Saturday or Sunday and see those cars for sale, long before they ever reached our distribution facilities.

"Throughout that first year we constantly did work on the design side," Frank Sesto said. "Within a few months it became very clear that while the little z-shaped torsion-bar axle was an incredible engineering feat, it was also a manufacturing nightmare. So we started to examine whether we could get that same initial performance with a straight axle, and what did it really mean in terms of performance. There were lots and lots of hours of testing, tens of thousands of distance runs. I remember statistically that the torsion bar, if everything was done properly, was certainly superior to the straight axle.

"After a while," Sesto continued, "we just said that we weren't getting as much out of the axles and bearings and that suspension as we were putting into them and we went to a straight axle."

Through that first Christmas production, the Hot Wheels car evolved so much it was almost a new product compared to what it was when Sam Djujic, Frank Sesto, and Gene Barker saw their first one in the huge empty warehouse.

The changes were subtle to the casual observer, but to Jack Ryan's R&D engineers and designers, it was an unending project of improvement or simplification. Engineers and designers devoted a large portion of their time to inventing new technologies and writing and drawing "Idea Disclosures," the first step toward a patent for their new axles, chassis, and wheels. At their best, these "improvements over prior art" performed better and were simpler and less expensive to manufacture.

The wheels were another evolving innovation that deserved attention. Bill Summerfield used a graphite-nylon hub on a synthetic thermoplastic rubber that could be injection-molded in an ordinary plastic machine. "You just needed something that would have a low coefficient of friction. Well, graphite and nylon will do that pretty well. Teflon maybe would be better except that Teflon won't take the abuse. They make nylon hammers, they don't make Teflon ones."

Delrin as a bearing material came into Mattel through Janos Beny, a model maker with aspirations to become a designer. Beny had taken a night school class on plastics at L.A. Trade Tech a year before Ryan asked him to make toy cars go fast. Delrin was one of few options at the time. At that time Beny had used it to sheathe guitar strings for a folding toy guitar project.

Like many others, that toy never reached production, but Delrin entered Mattel's engineering resources pool and waited patiently for Howard Newman to find a new use for it.

The first wheels, even before they were stamped to look like Harry Bradley's Redline Firestones, were made to look like the Firestone tires and Goodyear Wide-Oval bias ply tires, with fat, flat surfaces. It was an ironic choice, given the obsession with low friction, but it was a design based on faithful appearance to real tires. Howard Newman and his boss Harvey LaBranche applied for a patent on January 8, 1968, but Ryan kept his inventors busy and the second incarnation appeared with an inside raised rim similar to railroad train wheels. While these rims keep a train from slipping off the track and must be inches tall and fantastically strong, the purpose of the Hot Wheels variation was to reduce the contact patch to a narrow strip much less than half the tire width and barely ten percent larger in diameter. This drastically cut rolling resistance and maintained the appearance of fat rubber tires. A patent application for this improvement appeared just before Thanksgiving.

Howard Newman and Bill Summerfield worked in Ryan's friendly competitive atmosphere and each devised a shape that can best be described as a slice of a cone, a shape called

In the early days, Bob Rosas and others in engineering cast brass versions of nearly every Hot Wheels model before committing to production. Brass cars matched the weight of zamac, and so engineering ran them in test runs through banked turns, loops, and the Super-Charger. This brass, hand-painted Mongoose, completed for 1969, went through countless track runs before Mattel released the car based on Tom McEwen's dragster for production in 1970.

Designer Bob Lovejoy created a scorpion-inspired concept hot rod in mid-December 1971.

frusto-conical. The largest diameter of the slice fits against the inside of the car, and the angle of the cone is extremely shallow so that the tires still look fat, yet the innermost diameter supports the car to reduce what automotive engineers call its contact patch, the area of the tire in contact with the road, to four tiny points on the Hot Wheels cars. Again, the patent went to Newman and LaBranche.

In this highly charged creative atmosphere, accruing patents was a greater reward to the ego than the pocket book. As is the case nearly everywhere, objects invented on company time were considered company property. Staff inventors at Mattel were duly rewarded $1 for each patent, while all assignments and royalties went to Mattel. While most ideas remained secret until

Mattel launched Ira Gilford's Heavyweights series of concept trucks with the Ambulance in 1970. Visible beneath the hand-painted prototype decoration is the brass casting that engineering prepared to check the weight and the center of gravity of the new trucks.

97

ORIGINAL
HOT WHEELS
SOUND TRACK

Forward Records

Another element of the burgeoning Hot Wheels lifestyle for youngsters was this LP released by Forward Records. The record contained songs from the Saturday morning television cartoon that launched in the late 1960s.

Mattel filed the patent applications, an accident of coincidence exposed their secret earlier than intended.

With cars like a custom Camaro, a custom Firebird, a custom Mustang, a custom Cougar, and Harry Bradley's custom Dodge Deora and Custom Fleetside in the new product lineup, Elliot suggested that they call Detroit for design approval. Al Baginsky worked in R&D as a project engineer and moved toy ideas through design, testing, and other steps to turn them into projects ready for production. He was assigned to Hot Wheels.

"We got models of the first ten cars ready," Baginsky explained. "Because it was so confidential, my boss, Stan Woodward and I agreed that the cars going to Detroit [would] be built with a fat solid axle like the Matchbox cars. Detroit really didn't need to know about the fast wheels and our independent suspensions. My boss's boss, though, Harvey LaBranche, said, 'Hey, we can trust these guys. Let's put the correct wheels back in.'

This unpainted zamac body was a pilot production model assembled without interior or plastic windows and with mismatched, scrap wheels, to make sure the chassis would attach securely to the body.

The clear plastic sun roof was an early modification to the rear-loader Beach Bomb. This modification removed metal mass from the roof to lower the vehicle's center of gravity for the "loop test."

The addition of sidepods to the Beach Bomb solved the challenge of compatibility with the Super-Charger. This version earned the nickname "side loader."

Today, rear-loader Beach Bombs, particularly in pink, are highly valued by collectors.

The Volkswagen Beach Bomb from 1969 is one of the most collectible Hot Wheels cars ever made. Two versions were produced: the first, in limited quantity, with surf boards sticking out the back of the van, and the second with the boards stored in so-called sidepods. Both are valued by Hot Wheels collectors and Volkswagen enthusiasts alike.

THE VOLKSWAGEN BEACH BOMB

The 1969 Volkswagen Beach Bomb is one of the most interesting and collectible of the Hot Wheels Redline cars. Collectors debate for hours about the evolution of the variations of this car.

Mattel's first runs of the Beach Bomb were produced at the Hawthorne plant in 1969. The first batches to come down the assembly line were rear-loader models, in which two plastic surf boards were stuck through the back windows—for a real California beach effect.

What makes the story of the VW Beach Bomb so interesting is that, in its effort to reproduce Volkswagen's van faithfully, it succeeded too well. Just like the full-size vehicle, the model is narrow and top-heavy. Both of these traits created problems for the car when going through the banked turns and loops of Hot Wheels track and through the Super-Charger accelerator.

Part of the job of the factory's quality-control manager, Gene Barker, was to routinely pull initial production vehicles off the assembly lines and test them to be sure they rolled fast, far, and straight down the track. Later tests would check stability through curves and loops. After perhaps only three

or four dozen rear loaders came off the prototype line, some completely painted and fitted with interiors, it was clear the cars would not pass the test. Barker and his senior inspectors had the authority to stop production, and that they did.

Knowing that they had a potentially popular vehicle on their hands, Mattel looked to its ever-resourceful engineers to come up with a quick fix. They added metal mass to the bottom of the chassis in order to lower the van's center of gravity, greatly improving its ability to corner and complete the loops. But it still was too narrow for the Super-Charger.

Elliot Handler initially questioned whether every Hot Wheels car needed to go through every stunt, work with every accessory. He, Jack Ryan, and the other decision makers ultimately decided, yes, they did.

After resolving the center of gravity problem, engineering determined that the only solution to the Super-Charger challenge was to widen the van's body. Howard Rees and Larry Wood came up with "pods" to add to both sides of the van. The sidepods widened the van enough to work well through the Super-Charger, and also provided a nifty place to

store the surfboards. This additional metal mass down low improved cornering as well. Rees, Wood, and the engineers went through several test versions as they fine-tuned the sidepods' appearance and balance.

Along with the sidepods, Rees and Wood also redesigned the Beach Bomb to include a full clear plastic "sunroof." Along with the nice stylistic improvement, the removal of metal mass from the roof further lowered the vehicle's center of gravity, improving its ability to stay on track through loops and bends.

Known as the "side-loader," the Volkswagen Beach Bomb with sidepods was the version that went into production in large scale for 1969. Because Mattel assembled so few of the rear loaders, these are among the most valuable of all Hot Wheels cars. Prices often exceed $15,000 for a single van, as long as someone is willing to sell. Though the side loader version is considerably more common, this model appeals not only to Hot Wheels collectors but also to Volkswagen enthusiasts, so their value is still several hundred dollars for cars in perfect condition.

"For whatever reason," Baginsky continued, "but certainly an unfortunate coincidence, the Matchbox people were in Detroit at the same time, getting approval for their own designs. And they saw our axles. Elliot was fit to be tied. It was a huge blunder."

The accident of timing tipped Mattel's hand to Matchbox who, once they'd completed their rounds in Detroit, rushed home with glimpses of a daunting challenge. It would only get worse for Matchbox.

Mattel closed the production year at 4 P.M. Christmas Eve, and when Seymour Rosenberg did his sums early in the New Year, he found Mattel had produced slightly less than fifteen million Hot Wheels cars. They'd still lost money, but this was due to huge duplication costs as the staff in Hong Kong purchased machinery, acquired tooling, installed Ransburg painting systems, hired and trained several thousand more assemblers,

and struggled to get going. The Hawthorne plant had reached its million-a-week production goal in November, but it would be the spring of 1969 before Hong Kong got close to that number. By that time, Elliot and Ruth had attended the English Toy Show.

"They had an evening," Elliot recalled, "where they held a black tie formal dinner, and during the evening they awarded prizes for best toys in every category. It was our first year there with Hot Wheels cars, and when the hosts came to 'Top Toy of the Year,' they announced Hot Wheels. From the table behind us, we heard a big, loud, collective sigh.

"We turned around and looked. We had never realized it, but we had been seated right next to the Matchbox people. So there we were, as startups, and we had earned the English Toy of the Year award. They were very disappointed."

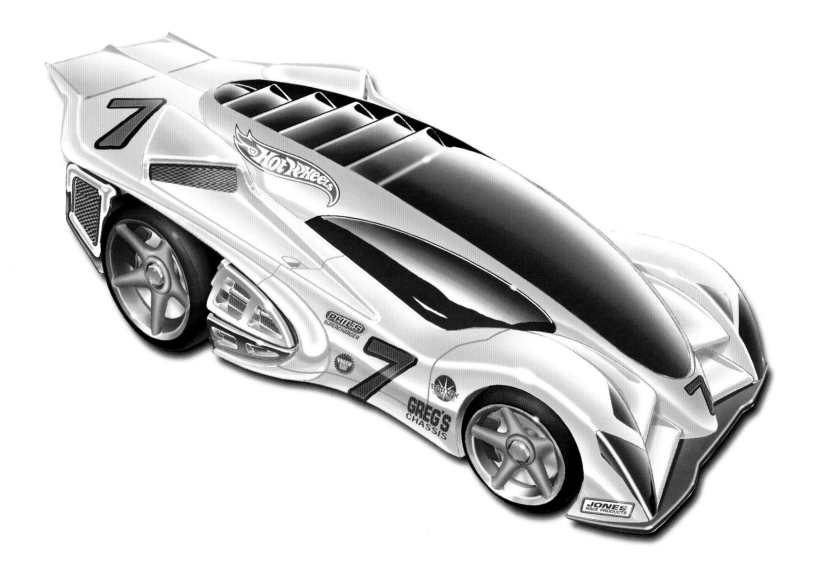

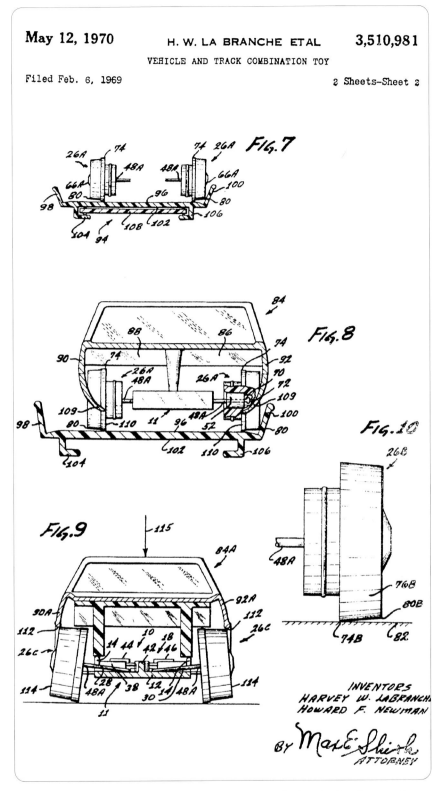

May 12, 1970   H. W. LA BRANCHE ETAL   3,510,981

VEHICLE AND TRACK COMBINATION TOY

Filed Feb. 6, 1969   2 Sheets—Sheet 2

INVENTORS
HARVEY W. LABRANCHE
HOWARD F. NEWMAN

BY Max E. Shirk
ATTORNEY

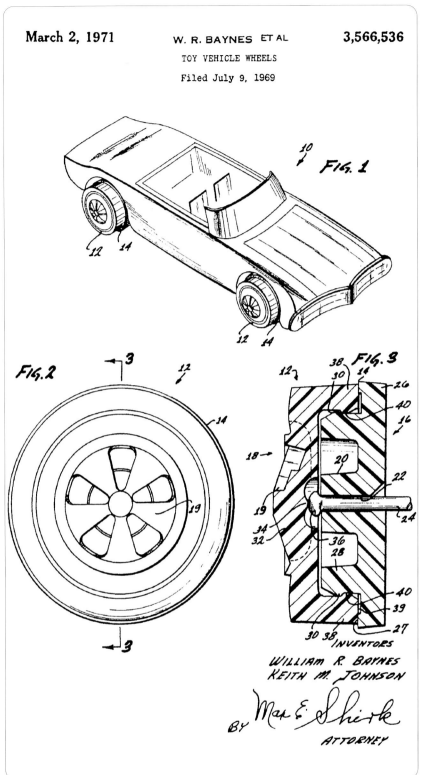

March 2, 1971   W. R. BAYNES ET AL   3,566,536

TOY VEHICLE WHEELS

Filed July 9, 1969

INVENTORS
WILLIAM R. BAYNES
KEITH M. JOHNSON

BY Max E. Shirk
ATTORNEY

Mattel filed its first patent application in November 1968 for its wheel and suspension system on the Hot Wheels cars. The wheel it illustrated held a constant outer diameter, putting a flat, fat "tire" surface on the track. As Howard Newman continued to work on it, he improved the system by shaving some plastic off of two-thirds of the width of the "tire tread," as shown in Figure 9 on the lower left. The fine wire axles acted as suspension working against the central tack points on the chassis. The next chassis improvement, illustrated in Figure 8, mounted straight axles under a long, flexible flat plastic plate. The biggest development, however, was the "frusto-conical" wheel shape, shown in Figure 10 on the lower right. To the naked eye, these wheels appear flat and fat. In fact, though, the contact point with the track is just a single point. Hot Wheels cars to this day use a wheel and suspension essentially like this one.

Engineers constantly tinkered with the wheel of the Hot Wheels car. Bill Baynes and Keith Johnson devised a Delrin inner wheel with a modified conical form that mated to an outer tire form that had the Redline stamped on it. This type of wheel, filed for patent in July 1969, was in use for nearly a decade.

8

A CRASH COURSE IN DEVELOPMENT
AND THE ECONOMY

The first recognition by Mattel of the value of Hot Wheels cars to a growing collector base was the Collector Club kit for 1970. The kit included three chromed cars: the Boss Hoss Mustang, Heavy Chevy Camaro, and King 'Kuda Barracuda.

As Hot Wheels cars matured, Mattel introduced the loop test. Gene Barker remembered these tests clearly. He performed tens of thousands of them in the first few years of production. Each car had to go through a 360-degree loop. Many vehicles failed because their center of gravity was too high. The Paddy Wagon and Volkswagen surf van would never pass that test.

"So now we had to decide: Will people expect their Paddy Wagon to run through the loop-the-loop? There were other products where the center of gravity turned out to be too high.

The relationship between the car's speed going into the loop and where its center of gravity was located determined if the car could get all the way through the three-sixty."

Flying off the curves was another consideration. Model maker/designer Janos Beny had taken a class in plastics and later he studied highway and road building at UCLA. He learned to calculate and develop bank angles and curve diameters for cars and trucks doing sixty-five or seventy miles per hour. That skill was invaluable when he designed track with turns for Hot Wheels cars that were doing a scale 240 miles per hour. Engineers such as Al Nash mastered high-speed cinematography to provide slow-motion analyses of Hot Wheels cars hurtling through loops, turns, and devices like the Super-Charger. This was a small house that straddled the track with two foam wheels that spun toward each other. As the car passed between them, it accelerated the Hot Wheels car. Early versions with smaller pads destabilized the cars, and Nash's films led them to develop larger, somewhat softer pads angled slightly downward. Powering the cars was a growing consideration. Slot car ideas prior to Hot Wheels had not worked, but then they tried buzzer cars.

"We had conceived a system," Marshall Pearlman explained, "using a rear-mounted buzzer in which the buzzer armature, as it rose and fell, turned a little gear that made the wheels turn. We powered them with AC and we had dual frequencies running on the track so you could race two cars. Then we had two frequencies for each car so you could steer them. We had a giant, complicated power supply, back when we didn't have transistors. We did this with brute force engineering and electronics."

Following the Buzzer cars, Mattel engineers developed a new series they called Zip Cars. Pete Folger from Advertising Research had been invited to speak to a group of men, and while his subject was to be the Mattel's entire product line, everyone in the room already knew about Hot Wheels cars. "They seemed to know everything, so I asked them what they'd think about Hot Wheels cars that could run uphill?"

The Zip Cars, introduced as the Sizzlers for 1970, came at a time of great creativity and staff expansion. Mattel hired a number of English designers and engineers who were attracted by pay rates almost five times what they made at home. Dennis Bosley and Derek Gable arrived within a year of each other, both from a film projector manufacturing division of J. Arthur Rank Corporation. Both Bosley and Gable went into Ryan's R&D groups.

"It was like being thrown into paradise," Gable recalled. "In Preliminary Design at the time, we had about eighty people. Mattel was among the first toy companies to have its own inside inventing and design groups. Elliot loved ideas and he'd get down on the floor and crawl around.

When it first appeared in 1968, this car was called the Custom Camaro. As part of the 1970 Collector Club kit, Mattel chromed the car and renamed it the Heavy Chevy.

In 1971, Mattel reissued several of the original cars from 1968, 1969, and 1970 under a new series name, the Spoilers. Mattel gave the cars new decoration and removed their hoods to show off chromed, supercharged engines. This car is the Boss Hoss, based on the Ford Mustang Boss 302.

Hot Wheels designers drew hundreds of cars every year. Larry Wood joked that he designed two cars by lunchtime every day. This rendition of racer Dan Gurney's Trans-Am series Barracuda never made it to production.

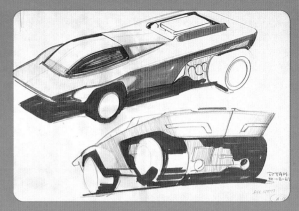

Paul Tam sketched this design for a concept Hot Wheels car. With some slight modification to the top of the engine compartment, it went on into production as a Sizzlers model, the Straight Scoop, in 1971. Sizzlers used tiny motors and rechargeable batteries for power.

SIZZLERS

Sizzlers appeared as the answer to a question that arose in a product planning meeting: What if Hot Wheels could go uphill? It was a question that provoked a flood of ideas. New track? New jumps? New accessories? But once again, the visionary Elliot Handler asked the next, all-important question: How would we do it?

Everyone in the room knew the answer. It would take motors. How to power the motors? Bill Summerfield remembered wondering aloud about a kind of slot-car system. Or could the cars have antennas off the front that brushed the sides of the track, which were the electric contacts? "Think about it," Elliot said to the group, and then he moved on to the next order of business.

The command "think about it" from Elliot Handler meant think about it fast and get me some ideas within a day or two. The room emptied, but few people went home that evening when quitting time arrived.

Several ideas and prototypes and creations were shared at the next product planning meeting, and one by one, Handler and Jack Ryan found faults. They didn't want children to have to buy a different track system. That eliminated electric-racer concepts

and slotted tracks between electric pickups. When George Soulakis suggested rechargeable batteries, the direction of the new product was set.

Internally, the design staff referred to the project as Buzzer cars. An early version buzzed angrily as it ran along the track. The naming lady, Carol Robinson, watched a prototype fly along the track making a sound that reminded her of food on a grill sizzling in the heat. Sizzlers were born.

Ironically, little in the way of accessories for Sizzlers ever sent them racing uphill. They were so fast—scaled speeds well in excess of 200 miles per hour—that their most popular accessory was the fat track, a nearly six-inch-wide black extruded sectioned track with a high, broad-banked turn that allowed cars to rise up above one another through the turns to pass. A charging station called the Power Pit and another accessory called the Juice Machine "refueled" the Sizzlers.

Handler and Mattel were pleased with the Sizzlers. Introduced in 1970, they remained in Mattel's catalog through 1974. Mattel reissued some of them in chrome in 1976 and gave them headlights for "night" racing in 1978.

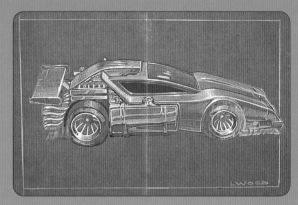

Larry Wood developed this Sizzlers concept in color. Before joining Mattel as a Hot Wheels designer, Larry Wood worked at Ford Motor Company, where he often produced design sketches and renderings in full color. This concept color drawing for a Sizzlers car led to the production model Long Count, introduced in 1978 during the second life of the Sizzlers series.

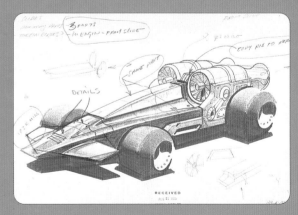

The outside contractor Industrial Design Affiliates (IDA) produced the block-and-shell models of Larry Wood's concept for the Co-Motion Sizzlers car. The drawing here shows red line notes referring to casting pieces and removable side-slides.

Engineers constantly experimented with ways to make existing products run faster or look different. This 1973 Sizzler, known as the Fire Works, has a number of unusual white plastic parts, including its pingpong-ball-style front wheels. In the production version, the engine and pipes were yellow, and it used five-spoke chromed wheels. The Fire Works was available in this pink color.

As Mattel's engineers worked out the mechanical logistics of making the Sizzlers go, they sometimes asked manufacturing to cast all the body parts in clear plastic. This allowed them to examine how each mechanical piece functioned in relation to the others. This clear model is of the Side Burn, which went into production for 1971 and was reissued as Side Burn II in 1976.

Product planners conceived of a next generation of Hot Wheels vehicles as a slot-car racing system, and they put engineers and designers to work on new cars as a variation of the un-slotted Sizzlers. This yellow prototype is based on the 1973 Sizzler Needle Nose. A flat peg below the front axle guides the car along the track. One major drawback, however, was that the peg's friction in the slot made the cars slower than Sizzlers, and the project burned out by 1973.

The Spoilers line introduced better sticker detail decoration to Hot Wheels cars. Typical of the Spoilers cars, this metallic blue King 'Kuda has no hood, so children and collectors can see the chromed metal engine inside.

This is one of Mattel's more popular collectibles named the Evil Weevil. Paul Tam created this car and Mattel introduced it in 1971 as part of the Spoilers line. Many Volkswagen enthusiasts still enjoy this twin-engined model as a fantasy design for the beloved Beetle.

"While Elliot and Ruth made every department feel they were essential to the success of Mattel, in Prelim Design, we knew we were the hub because we came up with the new toys. It was a very enlightened atmosphere. Fun was a part of the working environment. The permission to have fun yielded a lot of creativity in the products. It was sort of a permission to make mistakes. If you made a mistake, they viewed it as a stepping-stone to something that might be even better. If you came up with bizarre things, they just tried to make the bizarre thing useful as a toy that would sell."

To make Sizzlers cars move, mechanical engineer George Soulakis looked at every type of small motor available in those days. Mabuchi Motors, a Japanese supplier, made one called the SM02, but after testing it, Soulakis concluded it didn't have enough torque or acceleration, and it didn't have current drain low enough for a child to get a good amount of play out of it. So they bought some motors, changed the magnets, and revised the wiring and armature until they had what they wanted.

Powering Sizzlers cars developed out of Elliot's love of friendly competition. One group worked with a lithium battery. Soulakis

Ira Gilford redesigned the 1968 Hot Wheels Custom T-Bird for the Spoilers series in 1970. The new rendition was called the TNT-Bird. The racing number and stripe, the exposed chrome engine, and the small spoiler on the end of the car make it seem ready to explode down the track.

Light My Firebird, another "punny" name from the desk of Carol Robinson, is a Spoilers model from 1970. It was based on the Custom Firebird introduced by Mattel in 1968. It appears here in metallic blue.

This 1971 Spoilers model is called the Sugar Caddy. Ira Gilford designed it based on the 1967 Cadillac Eldorado coupe.

Hot Wheels collectors know this as the Jack "Rabbit" Special, but fans of Saturday-morning cartoons may remember it as the Bunny Car, the star of the Hot Wheels cartoon. First introduced in 1970, the Jack "Rabbit" Special was also adopted by the fastfood chain Jack-in-the-Box for a sales premium. Here the car appears in custom colors, reflecting a growing hobby among collectors. Known as Code 4s, these are models repainted either to commemorate an event or, in this case, to please the owner.

worked in Product Engineering, the group that took toy designs and made them production-ready. He knew they needed a self-sealing cell. One battery they looked at would rupture and leak acid if it was overcharged. "So I went to G.E.," Soulakis explained, "and they developed a double-A-sized Nickel-Cadmium battery with resealing capability. It was the first commercial use of a rechargeable NiCad battery in a toy. We developed the Power Pit,

a recharge station that gave the cars a forty percent recharge in just eight seconds." That solution excited everyone until the day Lenny Moquin brought in his own creation.

"He came in carrying a clear plastic bag with this pale yellow liquid in it," Gable recalled. "He had one of the little Mabuchi motors we were developing for the Zip Cars, and he'd put a propeller on the shaft. He told us he'd come up with a

This Custom Camaro included a stopwatch that could be used to time races on the Hot Wheels lap sets. Mattel experimented with producing a Hot Wheels stopwatch with a timing mechanism installed in any of several cars. The small weight of the digital timing mechanism affected the handling and performance of the cars, however, and Mattel feared that buyers might confuse the purpose of car and stopwatch. Instead, it introduced the separate watch, shown on the right.

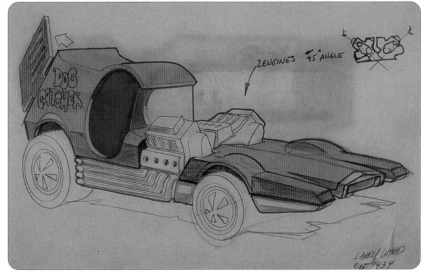

One of Larry Wood's earliest designs was his twin-engine dog-catcher truck. It went into production in 1971 as Mutt Mobile and was brought back in 1973 as Odd Job. This concept truck featured two engines canted away from each other at 45-degree angles. One wonders if Wood's experience chasing dogs was with extremely fast ones, thus the need for such engine power.

Ferrari's 312P first appeared at the 12 Hours of Sebring endurance race in 1969. With Chris Amon and Mario Andretti at the wheel, the car finished second overall in its first event. When Mattel introduced the Hot Wheels Ferrari 312P in 1970, the real-life car was in the prime of its competitive life. A rule change in 1972 forced Ferrari to abandon further development of the racer, and both Ferrari and Mattel discontinued the car in 1971.

new power source and it was virtually self-renewing. He called it the urine-air battery. We all looked at the baggie and cringed. 'It'll run forever,' he said, and he proceeded to demonstrate.

"We had suspended ceilings in our offices in those days and so Lenny climbed on his desk and hung the bag from some wires high up near the ceiling where everybody else in the other groups could see it. We were all thinking, 'Oh, God, don't drop it.' Next he hung the little motor up with its propeller. Then he fed the leads, a penny on one, a steel slug on the other, from the motor down into the liquid in the baggie and stepped down. The propeller started turning and it got up to a steady pace and it just kept going. Lenny got back to work and we just stood there. It was turning when we left work that night and all the next day and the day after. Guys in the other groups were doing all kinds of calculations, trying to figure out if this would work in these little cars or in any of the other electric power toys we were thinking about."

"It caused really a lot of excitement," Gable recalled with a laugh. "They started talking about patents, maybe even of inventing prizes, and so finally Lenny had to tell them. He had gutted the motor. We had fresh air and heating vents running above the false ceiling. He had cut a hole in the duct and poked another in the ceiling tiles and so long as the heating or air

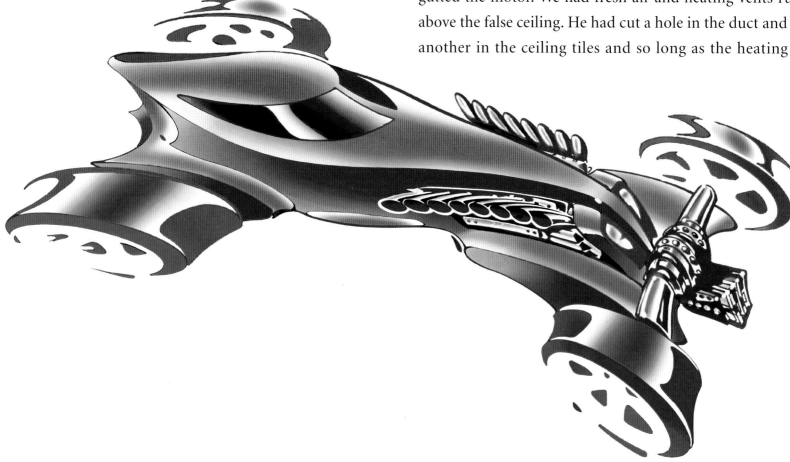

conditioning was on, and that was every day, his propeller would turn. It made the guys in engineering absolutely furious." The pranks were endless in those days.

After Ira Gilford left Mattel, the company hired a Ford designer named Howard Rees. He had been unhappy in automotive design at Ford and here he was doing more of it. His friend and former colleague Larry Wood also had left Ford and come to California to find work in the better climate. At a party one night, the two met again while Wood watched the host's children playing with Hot Wheels cars that Rees had brought for them. Wood and Rees compared notes and Monday Rees put in a good word for Wood as he put in for a transfer to the Matt Mason spaceman in boys' action figures. Wood was hired before the week was out.

Mattel introduced Sizzlers cars, first proposed and approved around December 1968, at the Toy Fair in 1970. Soulakis and others had developed race cars and dual-lane track sets. Using the same physics that Janos Beny had employed to develop bank angles and curve radius for the gravity cars, Soulakis determined that at Sizzlers-scale speeds, he needed a twenty-three-foot radius to keep the cars on the road.

"The problem was that you were going from a straight line into a very tight corner," Soulakis explained. "But because it was so tight, the cars wanted to accelerate up the turn and fly off. We tweaked it a little bit. The only time you really got in trouble was when you taped down the curves. If you don't tape them down, especially with Sizzlers, but even with the gravity cars, the curves move on the floor. You tend to lose all that energy because the force of the moving car moves the track as well. If you tape it down, you don't lose that energy and the cars tend to get through the turns faster. We did slow-motion photography to determine what was happening."

Mattel ended 1968 with back orders for millions of Hot Wheels cars. Financial optimists within the company believed those orders represented the tip of an immeasurably large iceberg

The 1/64th-scale Ferrari 312P was a champion just like the full-size racer. In order to promote Hot Wheels ownership and enthusiasm, Mattel introduced the Hot Wheels National Championship Derby in 1971. In Saginaw, Michigan, young Mark Judy entered his Ferrari 312P and won the regional championship. He took home a trophy that dwarfed the little red racer.

Mattel introduced the Peepin' Bomb in 1970 with an unpainted metal chassis. Early versions of the car, which was designed by Howard Rees, included a small tab in the passenger compartment that slid forward to hide the headlights beneath a black plastic cover.

This unpainted zamac Classic Nomad shows prototype wheels as Mattel began hinking about saving costs and deleting the red lines from Hot Wheels tires. Engineering experimented with a variety of plastics and compounds that might increase or at least maintain speed while reducing manufacturing costs.

Designer Larry Wood and design/engineer Bob Rosas were admirers of the American classic cars of the 1920s and 1930s. Product planning and marketing weren't convinced the classics would sell. Elliot Handler, a car lover himself, let Wood go ahead with his design for the "coffin-nose" Cord 812 convertible. Mattel introduced it in 1971 and it has become a valuable "Classic Hot Wheels" car. This 1/64th-scale epoxy block model of the car was fitted with wheels and painted for a photo for the 1971 catalog.

of demand for their new product. Ken Sanger's prophetic order for fifty million units had convinced executives that perhaps eighty million cars was not an unreasonable target for 1969, especially since Hong Kong approached a half-million-a-week production. Outside Mattel, the competition was bullish. Based on what it had seen in Detroit, Matchbox hurried its new series of Superfast models into production. The cars ran on fine wire axles and lightweight injection molded plastic wheels. Topper Toys introduced the Johnny Lightning cars, and a marketplace that couldn't get enough Hot Wheels cars in 1968 had more than enough options one year later. By 1970, even Mattel's Sizzlers were competition to the Hot Wheels gravity cars in an economy that tightened up by the time Christmas rolled around.

Below the surface, 1970 and 1971 were rough years for Mattel and for Hot Wheels cars. A fire at Mattel's warehouse south of Tijuana in the fall of 1969 destroyed much of the raw

Howard Rees' London Taxi reached production in 1971 as the Cockney Cab. This unpainted zamac pre-production model went through assembly to make certain that all parts fit correctly.

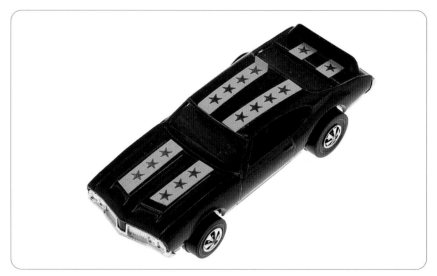

Larry Wood redesigned and re-proportioned Oldsmobile's 1968 4-4-2 coupe and introduced it as the Hot Wheels Olds 442 in 1971. The 442 was one of the early Hot Wheels experiments to include add-on stickers for decoration. The result was crude, as edges dried out and curled up over time.

Adolph "Eddie" Goldfarb brought his idea to Mattel in 1971. Elliot Handler and his marketing staff liked the FARBS that Eddie had created. Like many toys in the volatile toy industry, however, FARBS proved to be a one-year wonder, introduced for 1972 and gone by year's end. The two unnamed models in the foreground never saw production; the character in the rear became Hy Gear.

Mattel introduced FARBS in 1972, but the company did not consider them Hot Wheels. It called them instead "Fantastic Car Kooks." Elliot Handler wanted these models in production quickly, so his engineers fitted Hot Wheels redline wheels to each of them. This unpainted prototype is known as Hot Rodney. Rodney's head turned around completely.

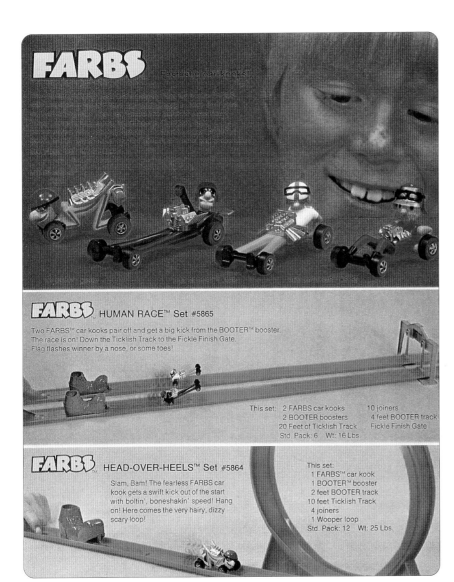

FARBS appeared in the Hot Wheels section of Mattel's dealer catalog in 1972, but they did not use any Hot Wheels identification.

Designer Tom Daniel of Monogram Models had created this funny-car-style school bus as a plastic kit. After acquiring Monogram and the rights to Daniel's designs in 1971, Mattel quickly turned out a Hot Wheels scale model of the S'Cool Bus as part of the Heavyweights line. This final prototype does not bear the S'Cool Bus logo on its sides, and the supercharger air intake is black plastic rather than orange as in the production version.

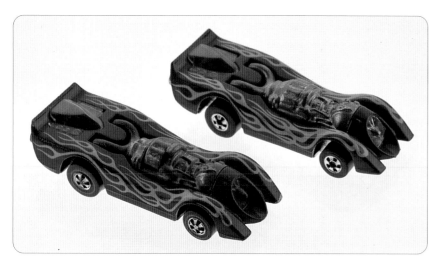

This pair of Jet Threat models shows a metallic magenta hand-painted prototype (foreground) alongside a regular production car. Hot Wheels car designers often used staff from the Barbie doll's prototype face-painting group to do one-off paint schemes on their car models. It routinely took these steady-handed artists three or four full days to complete one car for catalog or television commercial shoots.

This Strip Teaser car has a chassis and body made from zamac from an Australian supplier. The zamac had impurities, however, and while painting seemed to stabilize the metal, the unfinished, unpainted bases began distorting during the casting and cooling process. This instability continued to warp the base even after packaging and shipping.

Mattel's 1971 catalog highlighted the advantages of Hot Wheels cars over their competitors, including their "dynamic design," whether "authentic replicas or wild originals." The most important boast of all: "In the die-cast car world, they're the fastest set of treads on the track."

materials and a third of the Christmas shipments. Most retailers cancelled their orders to cut their own losses.

Less than six months later, Ruth was diagnosed with breast cancer and underwent an immediate mastectomy. She barely participated in the operation of the company for the next two years, despite being the real business brain behind Mattel's fifteen years of success. Then in the fall of 1970, a dockworkers' strike left ships loaded with parts and products for Christmas shipments stranded miles off the shores of Southern California.

By the time the strike was settled, even though Mattel assembled some product and got it shipped, it left another financial disaster as great as the Mexico plant fire the year before.

In 1970, Mattel acquired Monogram Model Co., and the work of its designer Tom Daniel. It also introduced the Hot Train, eleven more Sizzlers cars, and Earthshakers, a lineup of three battery-powered heavy construction toys, all designed by Larry Wood. Mattel produced these vehicles only in 1971. Designer

Though the car was officially called the Strip Teaser, collectors know it as a "crumbler" because the base of the car literally crumbles to pieces. In the early 1970s, Mattel contracted out to new suppliers for raw materials in order to meet the enormous production demands, and sometimes the product didn't live up to the challenge.

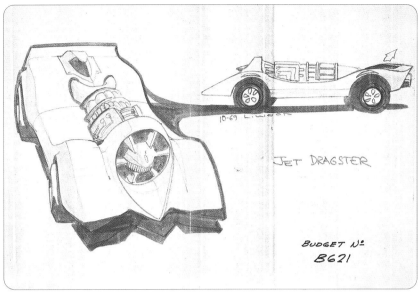

This blueprint copy shows Larry Wood's proposal sketch for his concept racer, Jet Threat. While the sketch is dated October 1969, the blueprint appeared soon after. Notice the original ink approval and budget authorization code. Jet Threat went into production in 1971.

Bob Lovejoy created Hot Birds, another one-year product, that were made up of six metal airplanes with retractable wheels. Lovejoy also designed the RRRumblers, a set of six three-wheeled motorcycles, which continued through 1974.

After "Namesmith" Alexandra Laird had taken time off in 1968 for an illness, she hired Carol Robinson. At year's end, Laird assigned Robinson the task of naming the new Hot Wheels models. Robinson began with the Volkswagen Beach Bomb, and Ira Gilford's Twin Mill and the Turbofire. Robinson, who worked similarly to Laird with a note pad and a thesaurus by her side, was dubbed "the naming lady," although Larry Wood always thought of her as "the punster."

Mattel launched Hot Wheels cars in 1968 with sixteen models in as many as fifteen colors. In 1969, it introduced twenty-four new cars, including the top-heavy Paddy Wagon and Volkswagen Beach Bomb. The VW had two surfboards stuffed through the rear window at first, and later they were mounted in pods on the side of the body to give the vehicle greater stability. The company followed in 1970 with thirty-three new vehicles and launched Ira Gilford's line of Heavyweights concept trucks, as well as two Harry Bradley/Howard Rees combinations that attached Rees' free-flying gliders and take-off ramps to Bradley's Deora and El Camino-based Fleetside. Robinson's humor was all over the lineup, from the Mod Quad to the Nitty Gritty Kitty.

Mattel had planned the 1971 line in early 1970, and brought out another thirty-five models. Most of them were designed by Larry Wood. The year's entire lineup of names came from Robinson who placed her tongue firmly in her cheek and never removed it. The year saw the first evidence of Hot Wheels involvement with drag racers Tom "the Mongoose" McEwen and his nemesis, Don "the Snake" Prudhomme. When marketing ran McEwen's proposal past Elliot Handler, he loved it.

"Either one of them or the other one always wins," he remembered saying at the time. "It was perfect for us because we were always on the winning car. And their rivalry excited their fans and put us in front of a huge audience."

At the end of 1971, Mattel posted its first-ever loss. As a result, for 1972, Mattel offered only seven models in the last of the Spectraflame colors, three of the vehicles in a single color only. In order to save another two cents per car, Mattel discontinued the collector buttons as well. The company introduced new product lines it had approved in 1970 and 1971. There were four new Sizzlers cars and a racing tricycle motorcycle line called Chopcycles. These lasted through 1972 and into 1973 before being discontinued. An outside designer, Adolph Eddie Goldfarb, brought in a lineup of four Fantastic Car Kooks that were somewhat bizarre-looking human caricatures with movable heads. They were completely conceived and engineered when they arrived on Mattel's doorstep. Mattel hurried these into production at a frantic pace.

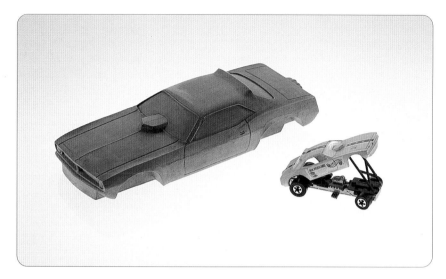

This epoxy block mold, made in Mattel's model shop by Stewart B. Renner in 1969, shows the solid form, four times enlarged or 1/16th scale, of the Hot Wheels version of Don "The Snake" Prudhomme's Plymouth Barracuda Funny Car. Mattel released the Snake in 1970, and reintroduced it as Snake 2 in 1971. The casting was brought back again in 1974 for another run of the Snake and Mongoose funny cars as well as for yet another model called the Top Eliminator.

Stan Christensen, the tool room foreman at Neward Die & Manufacturing, remembered making the first die-cast Hot Wheels bodies and injection-molded plastic chassis and working around the clock on a production schedule he recalled was break-neck.

Another product, Hot Shots, required its own race between prototypes to see which version would go into production. Derek Gable conceived a dragster with a wind-up motor. A child pulled the string to wind up the motor, and when it ran, it threw sparks.

"At the same time," Gable continued, "Gordon Buck, who was working for Jack Barcus' product development group, had come up with a dragster idea using flywheels for wheels. It was very clever. You revved them up using a piece of Mylar that was wrapped in a spool. You pulled it and kept pulling until it was revved up, then you put it on the track and it took off."

Mattel also looked at the Snake and Mongoose dragsters, but only had enough money to do one type. A fifty-foot race would determine which of the two was faster. "Gordon's car was very fast, but all its power was at the beginning. Mine, as it ran throughout the race, seemed actually to build up speed as it went. So we started the race. Gordon revved his up, it was a

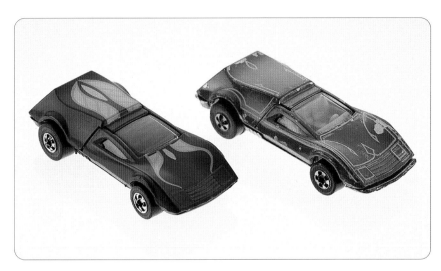

As information surfaced in 1971 and 1972 that Spectraflame paints contained trace elements of toxic substances, Mattel had Bob Rosas begin testing new paints. Here Rosas has painted the concept car Tri-Baby, introduced in 1970, in enamel green. When the model reappeared in 1973 as Buzz-Off, several versions displayed the yellow pinstripe tampo while others had the "beetle" design, shown on the blue car here.

'go,' he put his car down, and it shot off like a bat out of hell. It ran way ahead, and mine took off fairly fast, but it just kept going and his had started to slow. I think I won by less than a foot. It was really exciting and everyone screamed that it was a kind of tortoise-and-hare race. Elliot looked at the two of them and decided right then and there to put mine into production. I think Gordon was upset, and rightly so, because he'd lost by so little."

By the end of 1972, the enthusiasts delivered their verdict on Sizzlers. Buyers found the racing toys too expensive for too little playtime. While George Soulakis and G.E. managed to squeeze as much as five minutes run-time out of a ninety-second charge, the early NiCads had a strong tendency toward charge-memory and took whatever partial recharge was accomplished as a full load. Worse than that, the question of play value arose again when children complained that their only activity was retrieving cars that had flown off the curves.

In one of Ruth Handler's infrequent visits to Mattel during 1972 due to her battle with breast cancer, she met with Elliot, Seymour Rosenberg, Dennis Bosley (who took over Preliminary Design and R&D for Jack Ryan), Ray Wagner, and a few others. As she reviewed sales figures and projections for 1972 and 1973,

someone in the room wondered aloud if it was the end of Hot Wheels cars?

The room fell silent, everyone with their own thoughts. What was there to replace it? What was the next boys' toy? Apparently anxious to get on to the next subject, Ruth said, "Well, let's give it another year and we'll see then." In that year, Mattel attempted to improve sales and increase earnings. Some of those efforts changed the course of the Handlers' lives, and those of many others, for years to come. In the short term, Mattel laid off 2,000 employees worldwide before the end of 1972.

Shell Oil Company approached Mattel in 1971 with the idea of using Hot Wheels models as gas station promotions. For 1972, Mattel introduced a line of ten Zowies, tiny cars one-third the size of Hot Wheels cars meant to sell for forty-nine cents with a full tank of gas. Shell wanted real Hot Wheels cars for 1973, and with sales down and warehouse stocks growing rapidly, Mattel was pleased to release the Ferrari 512S; Bugeye, Jet Threat, and Strip Teaser, all Larry Wood concept cars; Howard Rees' Short Order and Peepin' Bomb; Ira Gilford's Splittin' Image and Twin Mill; and Bob Lovejoy's Rocket-Bye-Baby. In February 1971, the Organization of Petroleum Exporting Countries (OPEC) announced it would set the prices of its products. Oil companies faced an additional $10 billion in costs that they passed on to customers in an already wage-and-price controlled economy. Suddenly, discounted toys at Shell stations seemed inappropriate and Shell backed out.

For 1973, Mattel offered only three completely new castings. Shell's withdrawal had been one factor. Another part of the reason for this was the Hot Wheels line had lost designers and engineers to layoffs and transfers to other, still-successful products within Boys' Toys. Despite this, the Hot Wheels line expanded greatly from the 1972 offerings. Many of these "new" cars were simply previous-year castings reissued in new enamel colors. On top of these, Mattel added Revvers. This line of rubber band-powered die-cast vehicles, slightly larger than Hot Wheels cars, was a typical toy industry effort to keep new product before the buyers. While Hot Wheels sales began to improve through 1973, they were still far from Mattel's earliest expectations.

9

THROUGH THE GLOOM
AND INTO A NEW DIRECTION

Leave it to Larry Wood to create a hot-rod version of an English sports car. Here Wood followed in the well-trod footsteps of legendary car designer Carroll Shelby by installing a high-performance American V-8 engine in a nimble little Lotus Super Seven. Mattel introduced Wood's Lotus in 1974 as the Sir Rodney Roadster.

The first time George Soulakis saw pad printing, the tampo process from Germany, was at the National Plastics Expo in Chicago in 1972. "I came back and told my boss, Dennis Bosley, that I'd like to spend ten thousand dollars to do a few samples." Mattel had just promoted Soulakis to director of engineering for his development work with the Sizzlers motor and NiCad systems. His new role resulted from the reorganization process that moved the separate Hot Wheels division back under the bigger umbrella of Boys' Toys. He had worked with plastics and electro-mechanicals since 1963, and his visit to the NPE was a way each year to see old friends and learn new things.

Pad printing originated as a process to impress permanent inks onto delicate surfaces. Wilfried Phillipp, its inventor, opened his print shop doors in 1956 and strictly did industrial engravings in Kortal-Munchingen, Germany. Phillipp assembled his first pad printing machine in 1965, and by 1968, he had perfected the technique. With his sixty employees, he made presses that the Swiss watch industry embraced as a superior way to print watch faces. The earliest versions of Phillipp's machines were hand operated and pressed a slow-drying, oil-based ink onto the watch face with pads made from gelatin. In 1970 Phillipp showed the first commercial "tampon," or pad, printing machine at the Hanover, Germany, Print Fair

Designer Bob Lovejoy was ahead of his time. He drew up designs for things like this hot-rodded Conestoga covered wagon some thirty years before Mattel went ahead with production versions of shopping carts and coaster wagons and even toilet bowls with supercharged engines. This design, created in March 1972, was typical of Lovejoy's humor.

The blueprint version of the Hiway Robber shows IDA's red line modifications for their model makers. This drawing is dated November 1969, but Mattel didn't introduce the car until 1973, an unusually long delay between design, modeling, and production.

As George Soulakis and Bob Rosas developed the tampo-print process for Hot Wheels cars in 1972, they initially thought the printing process worked best on raised surfaces, such as the elevated "8" on the early prototype green El Rey Special. After learning that raised surfaces were not satisfactory, they experimented further. On the blue-body car, they tried numbers different from the engraving. The "1" here is almost unreadable when stamped over the raised "8," yet the printing itself held detail very well. This led Rosas and Soulakis to conclude that the best printing would result on flat surfaces, as on the example at the rear. Manufacturing revised the molds and Mattel introduced the El Rey Special, with tampos on flat surfaces, for 1974.

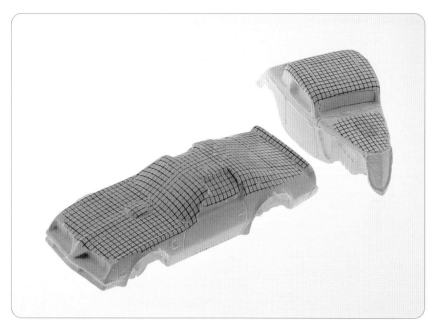

Through the many steps of the tampo-print process, one stage in its development on any new car is this grid overlay projection. These epoxy models of the 1978-introduced Hot Bird Pontiac Firebird and the 1980 model Ford 3-Window '34 show the tampo-print gridlines.

After Mattel had to discontinue Spectraflame paint in 1972 due to child-safety concerns, tampo printing restored visual excitement to the lineup. This production 1970 Demon displays the tampo-gridlines engineer Bob Rosas used to get decorative printing to work on the cars. Alongside the gridded Demon is the 1974 model, renamed the Prowler, for 1973, in green with tampos on the engine hood and roof. The Demon/Prowler was Mattel's replica of a famous show custom car called the L'il Coffin.

under his company name, Tampoprint, A.G. Within a year, Tampoprint had orders for 100 machines from Swiss watch and clock manufacturers and some German automotive instrument makers. The next year, 1972, Tampoprint booked floor space at Chicago's McCormick Place and hoped to entice manufacturers who used plastics to consider its process as a solution to the problems of printing on compound, complex surfaces.

"When I saw it in their booth in Chicago, they could type your name and print it around a pencil without distorting the letters," Soulakis explained. Tampoprint described its technology as "an indirect photogravure process in which they etch an image lightly into a flat printing plate. Jets flood special ink across the plate, and then it's scraped to leave ink only in the sunken etched areas. The machine rolls

a silicone-based rubber pad over the plate to pick up the sticky ink. Ink won't penetrate the rubber pad and when the pad presses onto the product, the ink releases like a film. The flexible pads can follow uneven, curved, or awkwardly-shaped surfaces. Because

Printing engineers from Tampoprint AG, the parent company from Europe, stressed the importance of projecting the decoration image accurately onto the compound curved and flat surfaces of Hot Wheels car. They developed the grid system, which Bob Rosas projected here on a green Baja Bruiser and the yellow body frame of the XT-3, a three-wheel racer concept car introduced in 1985.

Bob Rosas commissioned a tampo test on chrome-finished cars in mid-1974, after Mattel introduced Larry Wood's Sir Rodney Roadster earlier that year. Alongside it is a "Super Chrome" prototype of the Prowler. Super Chromes arrived in 1976.

This hand-painted prototype is known as the Baja Bruiser, introduced by Mattel in 1974. Model makers completed this truck for photography for catalogs and advertising; it is painted only on the passenger side. It appears here in the tampos introduced for 1982.

During the tampo-printing experimentation period, Bob Rosas and Larry Wood often created variations to see what decorations worked best. Two test variations on the 1972-issued Mercedes-Benz C-111 show different options of blue stars or a C-111 logo. The production version for 1974 included the tampo stars but no logo on the rear.

the ink is quick-drying, pad printing is suitable for 'wet-on-wet' printing, so multicolor designs are easily achieved in four-color printing processes." In other words, it was the perfect method to print on Hot Wheels cars. Dennis Bosley approved the sample project and Soulakis had a few cars printed. He then put together a proposal to buy the equipment.

"I talked to Frank Sesto in manufacturing, Josh Denham in operations, and of course, Bosley, all the V.P.s of the technical end of the company. I got them all to look at my proposal, to buy in. When I presented it to the company, with all those V.Ps in there, it was a done deal," Soulakis said with a laugh.

Mattel spent more than $100,000 on equipment. Part of the equipment went into Barbie doll production to stamp the eyes on the doll's face. Dave Edelson was the first one to develop pad printing inside Mattel. Frank Sesto sent the machines and Edelson directly to Hong Kong.

Tampo variations often tested designs or the abilities of paints and inks to adhere to bodies. Bob Rosas created these "He-Man" and "El Diablo Wants You" decoration schemes to evaluate paint and detail. Notice the Mattel staff names that appear on the El Diablo car tampo.

If what you see here confuses you, it should. Bob Rosas ordered these tampo evaluations for the Chevy Monza 2+2, but the only front hoods available at the time that matched the dimensions were those of the 1975 Mustang Stocker. Rosas ran a very small assortment through the tampo printer to check quality, thereby creating an unusual Mustang/Monza 2+2.

"This was a project that required one of my top engineers, Dave Edelson, to go to Hong Kong and stay with the project until he got it up to speed. He was there three months," Sesto explained. "We had bought certain offset printing equipment before, but now we had to go through and develop 'distorted art' to be able to transfer the decals we had previously used from a flat surface, as the artists designed them, to a contour surface.

That development was done here, by Bob Rosas and others, but it had to be implemented overseas. Just getting the machines set up was brutal."

Sesto made frequent visits to Hong Kong to check on the progress. "Dave would be covered from head to toe in ink. The machine spraying ink everywhere was just part of debugging the process. Dave then had to train the people to set up

Model maker Paul Peterson put in hundreds of hours carving the shell models of the Chevy Monza 2+2. Peterson signed the inside of the chassis base on September 11, 1974, adding the toy number (#7621). The Monza was introduced in 1975.

The Top Eliminator was a Larry Wood design based on drag racer Don Prudhomme's Plymouth Barracuda funny car, the Snake. Introduced in 1974, the car was available in blue, gold chrome, red, and white. Bob Rosas gave an early prototype a purple color as a test. After seeing Rosas' purple prototype, product planners decided not to offer a production Top Eliminator in that color.

Larry Wood stylizes his work when he's completing graphics packages, as shown in his rendering for Don "The Snake" Prudhomme's U.S. Army-sponsored funny car, introduced in 1978.

and run the equipment correctly. If you pad-stamp the car in-correctly, you've blown the cost of the die-cast, the paint, and the pad print." The accumulated cost that was already added to the product would be lost. Bob Rosas faced equal challenges back in California, though his were much less messy.

"When the technicians arrived from Germany, they told us we first had to put a grid pattern on our cars. That showed us where and how the lines stretched. So if we were going to print some-thing on a curved surface, we had to compensate the artwork. We literally stretched it, but in the reverse direction, especially if we had hard contours. On the sides of our vehicles, the lines could really stretch."

Rosas found outside vendors who took Larry Wood's deco-ration artwork and scaled it to four-times its life size, the same as all the wood-pattern models. "But we had them reverse it," he said. "If we saw the printed material was going to bend in one direction around a roofline or a trunk, we had to stretch it in the other way for the printing pads. That way, when we printed it, the lines came out straight, the words correct, the decoration in proportion. It was a process we had to learn."

At first they thought the numbers on race cars had to be raised, which would require all new dies. This would be more challenging to keep the print edges clean, so all of the rivets, door lines, and door handles were removed.

Larry Wood created this proposal sketch for a Ford Torino stock car. Though there is no date on Wood's drawing, Mattel put the concept into production in 1975 as the Torino Stocker.

These three versions of the Rodger Dodger, a 1969 Dodge Charger model that Mattel introduced in 1974, show the exciting variations in Hot Wheels details. The car normally appeared with a black interior, but the foreground plum-colored car has a prototype white interior. The test-color blue car in the rear is much rarer. Collectors pay as much as ten times more for it than the regular production plum, the white, or even gold chrome versions.

"We tried to see how much we could print on a car. We had a lot of racing sponsor decals. We had to first hand-paint the design on the car. Two women in the doll face-painting department who must have used a single strand brush, would paint all the detail, things like Pennzoil stickers, the Champion stickers, the Ford ovals." Hiroe Okubo or Marlene Dantzer did nearly all this. It would to take them as long as two full work days, and on the worst racing cars, it would take even longer to complete one prototype. Normally they painted make-up on prototype dolls and reddened the cheeks, lined the eyes to set the pad printing for Barbie doll or Chatty Cathy faces or others. They came to dread the Hot Wheels cars for all their detail.

"The pad printing process started out with a lot of experimenting," Rosas continued. "We printed things on cars that never went into production. On the production version of the Mercedes-Benz C-111 record car, we tried reversing tampos, putting blue where yellow was, yellow where the blue went. Only one exists like that, it was the kind of experiment where we found that sometimes colors worked in one place on the car, but on the same car, using the same combination of colors, they just wouldn't look right in another variation. It made us think about how we used color and did cars in the future."

The Classic Nomad was introduced in 1970 without any decoration. When Mattel reintroduced the stylish Chevrolet station wagon in 1973 as Alive 55, it added a Chevrolet logo and flame designs.

Mattel introduced tampo-printed cars for 1974, a year that benefited from the hard work of people like Soulakis, Sesto, Edelson, and Rosas. In the chemistry labs, Bob Piotto and his colleagues made similar advances, and when tampos appeared, so did Flying Colors, a new, non-toxic version of the Spectraflame paints that retailers and customers had loved through 1971.

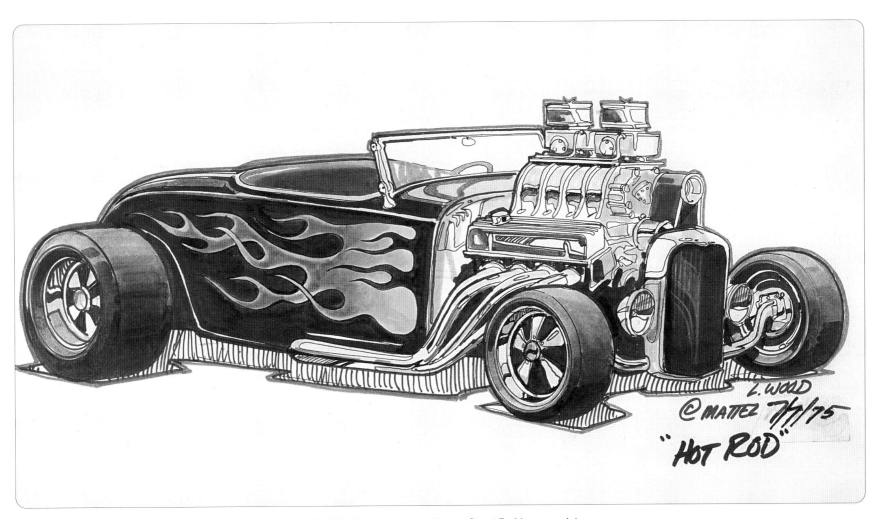

Larry Wood labeled this sketch "Hot Rod" when he drew it in July 1975. It entered production as Street Rodder a year later.

Almost as soon as Hot Wheels cars appeared, Mattel began giving away special, limited-edition versions of the cars. Such custom-painted models were given out to commemorate sales accomplishments or events. For Toy Fair early in 1975 in New York City, Larry Wood redesigned the white 1975 Super Van. Celebrating the success of the new Flying Colors paints with Hot Wheels toy buyers, Mattel produced about 200 of these vans for its top customers and sales people. A smaller group received chrome models similarly decorated.

In the mid-1970s Mattel was considering a licensing tie-in with Yamaha motorcycles. The art department hand painted the logo and design on the side of the Super Van for evaluation and photography purposes. Soon after completing this prototype, the licensing arrangement fell through.

This chrome Monza 2+2 was created as a gift for the department managers at Mattel's annual Christmas party in 1975. Larry Wood designed the Mattel Managers Association "MMA'75" logo on the roof as well as the "Winter Ball" and Santa Claus tampo decorations on the hood. Mattel produced just 200 of these commemoratives.

Mattel issued the 1957 Chevy Bel-Air in 1977. During 1976, carvers in the model shop produced this four-times enlarged (1/16th scale) wood model, from which pattern makers, using a pantograph to reduce the scale, made the metal molds for 1/64th scale.

For catalog purposes, Mattel needed painted versions of the Mustang Stocker, introduced in 1975. These two prototypes were painted by hand to give product planners a chance to review decoration options.

The Large Charge was designed to suggest an electric-powered concept car. Larry Wood first conceived it in 1973, and it was released in 1975. As it neared production, Bob Rosas supervised the hand-painted electric-circuit design that was eventually tampo-printed onto the rear deck.

"It was the reintroduction of brilliant colors," Rosas said with a laugh, "and the beginning of the resurrection of Hot Wheels from its doldrums in 1972 and 1973. Once we perfected the Flying Colors and the Tampoprint process, we went all-out with our advertising. Prior to that, we were dying."

"Alternate colors" first appeared in 1974, and was the result of cost-cutting and cost-saving efforts in Hong Kong. Bob Rosas watched it happen often, and occasionally requested it himself.

"We did trials cars. One time I was working in Hong Kong and I asked the line manager to move a car from the yellow paint line to the orange line where they were doing another car. I thought we may want to do that first car in orange the next year. We never did, but we made about a dozen of them just to see how it looked.

"Then sometimes we would do the normally red Corvette in blue. We did that because a line was running smoothly in blue paint. Can we keep a line running if we run the car in an alternate

Larry Wood drew this Model-T Ford hot rod in early 1976. It went into production as T-Totaller in 1977.

color? We'd telex Mattel and by the time they'd approve it or veto it, we may have run 5,000 cars. Well, if they looked good, they'd go ahead and distribute them." By 1972 and 1973, tooling, patterns, and other costs for a new casting were averaging $20,000 per car. Investing $120,000 or $140,000 in a less successful line was a tough decision in a business that required Mattel to replace more than half its product line each year.

It was a slow resurrection. Mattel introduced only seven new castings, more than either of the two previous years, and it added eight castings to the line that also had been given plastic engines or interiors or elaborate Tampoprint decoration. The catalog looked full and the cars shined much brighter, but at the year-end count, Mattel had sold only 3.5 million Hot Wheels cars, RRRumblers motorcycles, and Zowies mini-cars combined. Inside Mattel, some billing techniques had caught the attention of the Securities and Exchange Commission. Ruth Wheeler remembered this period in her book, Dream Doll: The Ruth Handler Story. She found herself in the center of a storm with many Mattel officers avoiding her. "The one person," she wrote, "who would talk to me eventually was the independent special counsel Mattel had hired to perform an internal investigation—a requirement the SEC had insisted upon..." Mattel sensed Wall Street's nervousness. In Hot Wheels engineering alone, six department directors lost their jobs.

This model of the '40s Woodie, made from hard rock maple wood, is shown with a production model of the Hot Wheels car from 1982 as well as the 1997 reissue. The reissue included two inverted surfboards on its roof. This model commonly was available as part of a Target "Motorin' Music" 4-car pack.

Bob Rosas used the El Rey Special as a test bed for a variety of tampo-print experiments and evaluation. The El Rey Special was introduced in 1974, and it re-emerged in 1976 as the black-bodied Formula P.A.C.K. racer.

The Hot Wheels model shop carved these preliminary wood and resin models of motorbikes in June 1976. In their finished form, these motorbikes fit into the rear bed of the '56 Hi-Tail Hauler, introduced in 1977.

The Mega-Fighter bike was conceived as part of the Mega-Force military vehicles series that Mattel launched in 1982. Even though it went through the model-making process, and production even completed raw prototypes, Mattel decided against producing the bike.

"Those times were really awful," Steve Nelson recalled. He joined Mattel in 1967 in package design and had worked with Ralph Parris on the blister cards and Rick Irons on the logo. Now these people and many others were gone. "Arvin Carlson was my V.P. of packaging. They put us on hold at one point. The entire company was going down. Then a future mayor of Los Angeles came in with a few of his friends, put some money into the company, and this enabled us to get back on our feet again."

Mattel consolidated a lot of the design and development areas, and laid off many people in the process. The employees finished their work by noon every day, so they devised other things. They started to do freelance work from Mattel for other companies. Nelson and Carlson designed the American Express card out of the design department of Mattel in the early 1970s.

Despite a shaky financial footing throughout Mattel corporate, company President Ray Wagner authorized twenty-three new Hot Wheels models for 1975. When Mattel learned that providing the same car model in unexpected color combinations had sparked buyer's interests, it made the policy unofficially official. On one of the models, a tow truck called the Ramblin' Wrecker, Larry Wood inaugurated a practice of personalizing the cars and trucks that continues to this day. This one gave him an unexpected surprise.

On the original 11-by-17-inch B-sheet drawing for the vehicle, he'd written in the logo, "Larry's 24-Hour Towing" along the side of the tow bed and added a phone number above it. He showed the design in the Marketing Design Review (MDR). "That's where everybody approves it, all the big shots," Wood explained. "Then we go into another meeting and if they approve it, we're a 'go,' and we just start rolling them out at that point. Every month we go into CA, concept approval, and then EA, executive approval. Concept was for price, executive approval was for final colors, how much

chrome goes on the car." Once these groups approved the design, he thought nothing more of it for months as the truck worked its way through production engineering. He still routinely drew at least two cars before lunchtime every day, and Larry's 24-Hour Towing was ancient history to him by Christmas morning.

At his home, the phone rang early. Convinced it was a wrong number, Wood answered it anyway. "Is this Larry's Towing?" a little voice asked. "What?" "Do you know your phone number is on my tow truck?" the little voice continued. "Where are you calling from?" Wood asked, and a flash of memory shot through his mind. To fill the space on the side of the tow truck, he'd drawn in his home phone number. "New Jersey," the little boy said. "Well, you should hang up now before your mommy and daddy discover that you're calling long distance to California." Within days, Larry changed his home phone number and redesigned the Tampoprint for the side of the truck.

Larry Wood redesigned and reproportioned Dodge's 1970 Hemi Challenger to create this Dixie Challenger. Mattel introduced the car in 1981 with U.S. production. These drawings, dated January 19, 1982, went to Malaysia, where production on the Dixie Challenger began later that year.

By that December, things were almost as bleak at Mattel as they could get. Pressure from the Securities and Exchange Commission investigations brought in new board members and additional auditors. Their actions and recommendations devastated co-founders Ruth and Elliot Handler. In the spring, as she recalled in Dream Doll, "In spite of my lawyer's advice to hang in there, I packed up my personal belongings and walked out of Mattel's doors for good." Elliot, whom everyone knew as the genius behind so many toys, found his heart was no longer in the place and, as Ruth wrote, he "followed about six months later." As Mattel faced a huge reorganization, it put its headquarters up for sale.

"There was a sign in front of the building," Larry Wood remembered. "The building was empty. The parking lot was empty. I was working on a floor with literally four other people. There were just five of us in Hot Wheels, on the whole floor. You could park in executive parking now because there were no executives anymore. The company was gone. There was nothing left."

Almost defying credibility, the strategy of broadening the Hot Wheels line and other Mattel products through that tough year turned the corner. As Ruth Handler explained in her book, *Dream Doll*, the company reorganized yet again. "The executives had written off nearly everything they could, inventory, tooling, accounts receivable, as losses. Much of the written-off inventory they sold at a discount," she explained, "sometimes at deep discount, but other times near full price, all of which they later reported—properly—as profit. The tooling produced more merchandise. Some of the accounts receivable they'd written off ended up being paid. And so, they had profits."

For 1976, the year of the American Bicentennial, Mattel produced two flag-decorated truck models that were painted red, white, and blue with pad-printed stars, as well as a Formula 5000-type race car similar to what inaugurated the Grand Prix car race in nearby Long Beach. Mattel also launched a line of eighteen Super Chromes including Rock Buster, a Baja-type dune buggy, and a reissue of Ira Gilford's Twin Mill, both as part of a package of six cars. The conversation Larry Wood witnessed about saving money on the red

Larry Wood designed the "RJ Rescue" vehicle in 1977. It joined the Hot Wheels lineup as Spacer Racer in 1979.

striped tires began to materialize in 1976. While a number of the reissues for the year rode on Redlines, about half the line appeared on black-wall tires. It was the first year a variety of wheel types were in the lineup. Mattel brought Sizzlers back with thirteen models, as well as play and track sets. This gave proof to the toy industry adage that—unlike *adult* products where once they're dead, they're gone—in the children's toy industry, a new audience is born every year.

"By 1976, we'd been manufacturing Hot Wheels cars in Hong Kong since 1968," Richard Caslow recalled. "But at this point, we were trying to dramatically increase running rates." Mattel transferred him to Hong Kong that year as Engineering Manager. He remained there for five years. "We were at 600,000 cars a week when I got there, and we were trying to get up to a million. The move up was primarily going to take an increase in equipment and an expansion in the facility, more tooling, more equipment, but we sure thought that was a lot of cars at the time. A million a week!"

In 1977, another era of Hot Wheels appearance came to a close with the last of the cars fitted with redline tires. A new product for that year was the Pro-Control Day/Night Challenge Sizzlers set with working headlights. In an unusual addition to its die-cast lineup, Mattel introduced a GMC motor home, which brought engineer Bob Rosas an interesting set of challenges.

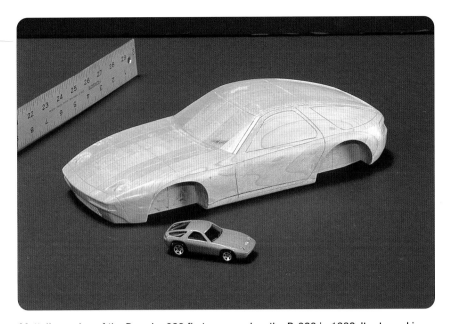

Mattel's version of the Porsche 928 first appeared as the P-928 in 1982. It returned in 1984 as Predator and in 1985 as Nightstreaker. Mattel resurrected the model in 1997 for a Porsche 5-Pack, in which it appeared as the green car shown here, alongside the wood model at 1/16th scale.

The Italian Fiat Ritmo/Strada economy car was introduced for European distribution in 1983. Mattel manufactured the model at its factory in France, but never offered it in the United States. The popularity of this automobile throughout Europe made it a very popular choice for a Hot Wheels export-only product. This is the 1/16th-scale epoxy model of the car.

"Had we made this motor home to the same scale as the cars, we would have had it sticking way out of the blister pack on both sides," Rosas said. "GM gave us the plans. The prints were huge, life-size. I had to scale this thing down. I wondered where am I going to take so much length out of this motor home and still have it look like a motor home? We took more than ten scale feet out of the middle and the end of this thing. Now it's the same size as the Corvette, in 1/64th scale, but taller, of course. We produced a set of gold models and gave GM a lot of them."

Mattel brought out a dozen new Hot Wheels vehicles in new blister packaging for 1978. The new packaging included cloth patches to match the seven groups of vehicles: Super Streeters, Drag Strippers, Oldies But Goodies, Rescue Team, Classy Customs, Speedway Specials, and Heavies. Unlike the earlier badges that Mattel packed in with the cars, buyers and collectors had to send for them. It was a renewed effort at getting back in touch.

It seemed to Wall Street that the worst was over not only for Mattel, but for the U.S. economy, even though national economic growth was still very slow. Retailers began to feel confident for the first time in several years. Toys 'R' Us revived its program of employee stock options during 1978.

For 1979, Mattel continued the seven series with patches, but it expanded the lineup to eighteen new models. In addition, Mattel introduced a set of Marvel comic character machines called Heroes, and The Scene Machine, a van or motor home with a tiny hole so the child could see a small photograph inside.

Mattel introduced its Hi-Rakers in 1980 along with a concept racer called Turbo Wedge, a 1963 Split-Window Corvette Stingray coupe, a 'Vette Van, a Dodge D-50 pickup truck, a 1940 Ford Woodie wagon, and a 1934 Ford three-window coupe. Although Mattel and inventor Gabriel Marason earned the initial patent for the Hi-Rakers idea in 1973, at that point it was to simulate real vehicles in appearance, function, and operation. While hot rods with raised rear body work had been around since the 1940s—the term "hot rod rake" applied to that low front-end, high back-end treatment—the Southern California car culture in the 1970s had taken it one step further with driver-controlled, on-board hydraulics that raised and lowered the entire car or any corner at the whim of the driver. Marason aimed to provide a Hot Wheels toy that reproduced this new trend. The car pivoted on the front or rear axle and was held in place by clips that anchored just ahead of and just behind the interior.

Larry Wood's drawing for the '37 Bugatti Royale, first produced in 1981.

The other new vehicle line for 1980 was Workhorses. This was a series of heavy-duty cargo trucks. Mattel also offered a group of four Caterpillar-licensed bulldozers, forklifts, dump trucks, and wheeled front-loaders.

By the early 1980s, Mattel had realized that its Hot Wheels cars were becoming valuable as something collectible. Ironically, Elliot Handler's toy, for which play value was critical and high speed was part of its definition, was becoming something older buyers acquired to put on their shelves and admire. Mattel recognized this new trend and potential market and issued its first collector's handbook, available only in a special three-car pack.

In an engineering response to increasing competition from other die-cast scale cars, Mattel introduced the Hot Ones and used new gold wheels on the fine wire axles from the late 1960s. Larry Wood's concept racer Cannonade inaugurated the line. With this group on the market, Mattel reclaimed the title of fastest non-powered die-cast metal cars.

Matchbox, the makers of the cars that had inspired Elliot Handler to compete in the die-cast market, was struggling at this time in the face of competition and the high labor costs of producing die-cast toys in England. After Matchbox filed for bankruptcy in 1981, a number of businesses, including Mattel, came to look at the toy company. Mattel already had added Corgi to its line in the previous years. The legendary Matchbox, with its scale and its loyal following, seemed a perfect fit.

"The reason Matchbox fell into financial trouble," explained Richard Caslow, Hong Kong's engineering manager, "was they were still manufacturing in England, which made it a very expensive proposition compared to doing it in Asia." Mattel sent Caslow and others to look over the operation in England. "I think their product was fine, but their major problem was labor costs."

"By the time Matchbox came available," market researcher Len Mayem recalled, "I was out of Mattel and had my own business. I had met David Yeh, knew him, visited his factories in the Far East. He owned a factory in Macau that made die-cast cars. He knew how to do them and he already had some equipment. He was looking to acquire companies which would use his factories for production. I suggested he look at Matchbox."

Yeh bought Matchbox and promised the British government he was going to keep it in England. Two weeks after the sale went through, he moved the whole operation to Hong Kong. Then he found out that all the English machines he brought to Hong Kong wouldn't run because there was a different electric current. Yeh had to rebuild all the Matchbox machines, which put him out of production for five or six months.

"This is typical of the nature of the toy business," Mayem added with a laugh. "Toy manufacturers have always been on the cutting edge of idiocy. In many cases, we're trying to do things we weren't able to do, we just didn't know it." For Mattel, the goal was even higher production while reducing costs.

"The move to Malaysia began in 1981," Richard Caslow explained, "and it was to increase capacity and at the same time, to control costs. In Hong Kong, they were becoming very high, so the matter of us moving was a matter of more affordable manufacturing as well as much-increased capacity. We looked at Shanghai as well, but at that point, manufacturing near the Hong Kong area was much easier to do than in Shanghai. That was still kind of a bureaucracy-ridden area in those days."

While the economy in the U.S. moved into another recession in 1981 and 1982, there seemed to be no evidence of that in the new Hot Wheels product line. Mattel issued fifty-one models for 1982, and twenty-three of the vehicles were new releases.

Mattel introduced Real Riders tires in 1983, another acknowledgment of a toy market that didn't have to roll as far so long as they looked good. Mattel understood that for something special, enthusiasts and collectors might pay more than $1 for a car. This opened up options to add value to the cars.

"We created the Real Riders tires," Bob Rosas remembered. "Another manufacturer was doing real rubber tires, but their cars were race cars. Ours definitely were not. No way were Real Riders going to race down the tracks. They rolled, but not very far. Rubber tires were for looks and when we accepted that, we took it one step further.

"We actually took a real tire and copied the tread design and we added the Goodyear logo. Our hubs were either white or silver. I wanted to chrome-plate them, but that was another penny and that put us over the edge on costs. Mattel decided to sell Real Riders for the same price as regular Hot Wheels cars, but we were paying the premium cost to do it."

For 1983, Mattel had a huge product spurt with ninety-six models including twenty new ones. The Real Riders appeared and Mattel introduced a new series called Extras. Children and collectors could modify and personalize these vehicles from the assortment of additional parts within the blister pack.

As the U.S. economy emerged from recession in late 1982, the traditional toy industry was under assault. Hand-held video games, computer play stations, and the spread of video cassette recorders meant that play time was becoming a distraction rather than an active experience. Barbie dolls and Hot Wheels cars kept Mattel afloat even as its own efforts with electronic games failed. Within the Hot Wheels brand, the new direction, hinted at with the premium-priced Scene Machines and the specially featured Real Riders, offered new growth. Hot Wheels cars were becoming collectible

10

INCREASING THE PACE,
IMPROVING THE PRODUCTS TO BET ON THE FUTURE

As a prototype, the Troop Convoy appeared in more vivid colors than its 1984 production versions. Mattel released the car in khaki, olive drab, or light blue. This patriotic color scheme never made regular production. Both of the red plastic tops shown here were removable.

Luis Montes de Oca had no experience with toys before Mattel. He joined the company in 1984 and worked for the Samples department, a small offshoot of Marketing. "I got it pretty quickly because I liked it, I enjoyed it. It was fun. I remember the first few months that I was at Mattel, in the old building along the 405 freeway. They had this place at the rear of the building called the back bay where the trucks used to load and unload. Next to this were the big trash dumpsters."

There was a room inside the Samples department called the Premium Room where the prototypes for Hot Wheels, Barbie, and preschool toys were stored. The room filled up rather fast because Mattel made a lot of toys, so Montes de Oca's bosses told him to throw away the prototypes.

For Mattel, 1983 had been a rough year outside the Hot Wheels and Barbie divisions. It was still reeling from the rough economy in 1981 and 1982, even though Mattel's sales growth exceeded 70 percent in the span between 1980 and the end of 1983. It barely fended off bankruptcy for the second time in a dozen years. While its share of the total toy industry consumer sales rose from 7.5 percent in 1980 to 11.9 in 1983, at the close of business in January 1984, Mattel reported a loss of $394.1 million and a negative net worth of $136.1 million.

It was another chapter in Toy Business 101, a roller-coaster ride graduate program without a textbook. Art Spear, an executive hand-picked by Ruth and Elliot Handler in 1974, started just as Mattel's first legal and financial problems approached

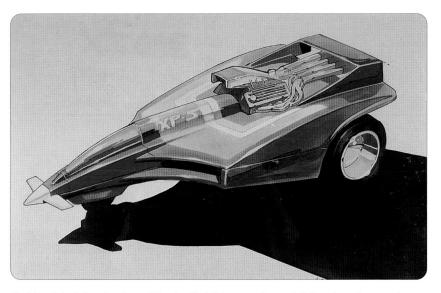

On his original drawing, Larry Wood called this supercharged delta-winged concept tricycle the XP-5. It went into production in 1985 as the XT-3.

This wild four-wheel-drive vehicle, drawn by Larry Wood in July 1984, became the Gulch Stepper when it went into production for 1985 release.

This is the epoxy block model of the sleek BMW M1, four times the size of the Hot Wheels car. Mattel first introduced the car under its own name in 1983, appearing throughout Europe and in Canada as well. It came back in 1984 as the Wind Splitter, as one of the Ultra Hots, with Mattel's newest free-rolling wheels. Through the early 1990s it alternated using the M1 and Wind Splitter names. In 1993 the M1 appeared as one of the Tattoo Machines, with graphics showing a growling German Shepherd.

This is the resin shell model of the Sol-Aire CX4, a racer that looks to many like the legendary Porsche 956. Larry Wood restyled and re-proportioned the Porsche racer that Mattel introduced in 1984 as #5902. The second number visible on some of the pieces shown here is the casting number. This is four-times larger, 1/16th scale, than the actual Hot Wheels car.

meltdown. Spear disliked and distrusted the toy industry and set a goal to bring toy revenues down to just half of Mattel's corporate income. He bought Western Publishing and the Ice Follies and ventured into the home security industry at a time when Columbia University MBAs were taught the mantra: diversify. Spear's diversification into Intellivision video games, Aquarius home computers, and other electronics weren't strong enough to handle that industry's shakeout in 1983.

The new disaster was largely due to a huge failure in Mattel's consumer electronics effort that lost $402 million in a single year. For the second time in a little over a decade, Mattel stock fell to below the price of a basic Hot Wheels car. Just as one investor

Mattel introduced a new Hot Wheels lineup for 1986 called Speed Demons. It offered six new models. Three more of these creatures joined the lineup for 1987, and 1988 saw the final two appear. This particular epoxy prototype never made production although other animal-based vehicles reappeared in 1996.

By 1987, the range of Hot Wheels vehicles was quite wide, extending from Speed Demons shaped like sharks to Ferrari Testarossa supercars to Quad-Runners. While Mattel introduced just 12 new models for 1987, it carried over another 26, bringing the entire lineup to 38.

group did with its $50 million infusion a decade earlier, another group led by John Vogelstein arrived in June 1984 with a $231 million rescue plan. Once again, Mattel stepped back from the brink. Over the next few months, Mattel returned to the core businesses that had survived two near-bankruptcies.

Mattel introduced eighteen new models into the Hot Wheels lineup for 1984, keeping the total number at ninety-six. Among the new models were the 1965 Mustang convertible, Baja Bug, Blazer 4x4, Blown Camaro Z-28, a Real Riders concept Dream Van, an Ultra Hots Flame Runner concept car, an Oshkosh Snowplow/Dumptruck, and a Phone Truck with a yellow plastic cherry picker.

For 1985, Mattel revisited military vehicles with two tanks, Big Bertha and Command Tank, as well as a Jeep, a Super Cannon concept vehicle that mixed a Baja racer with armor, and a half-track called Tank Gunner. In all, there were fifteen new models. Inside the company, 1985 was remembered as another year with big layoffs, but outside, it was the year that collecting Hot Wheels cars and gathering information about them took a very serious up-turn in the San Francisco Bay area.

Gourmet-food vendor Mike Strauss first noticed Hot Wheels cars when he got them with gasoline at Shell stations in 1972. A few years later, he noticed these same cars commanding respectable prices at toy shows. As someone whose work keeps him

on the road visiting his customers, he noticed a growing interest in the cars everywhere he went. Strauss was one of the first individuals to contact Mattel specifically to connect with engineers such as Bob Rosas and designer Larry Wood. His questions to them revealed a man with a vast interest and curiosity. Along with a friend, Russ Looker, Strauss founded the *Hot Wheels Newsletter* to spread accurate information about the designers, the cars, and their growing values to collectors. A year later, Strauss staged the first Hot Wheels collector's convention.

"Our first convention was in Toledo in 1987. We had a hundred people and charged them a dollar per ticket. You know," he

Larry Wood drew his Volkswagen Beetle in November 1987. It went into production as the VW Bug in 1989.

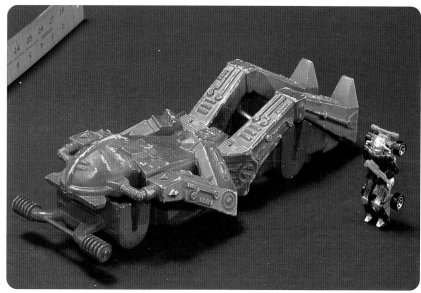

This is the Zombot with its chassis beneath it. This reclining robot carried a gun and was part of the Speed Demons line. Shown beside it is the 1996 production version. The Speed Demons line included other robots, snakes, sharks, bats, gargoyles, and lizards all on free-rolling Hot Wheels chassis.

recalled while walking the halls of the Sixteenth Annual Convention in 2002, "fifteen, sixteen years ago, people liked the cars, but it wasn't until the conventions that designers began to appear. Bob Rosas came to the second one, and then the car took on an identity. 'This guy designed that car, these too!' We began to be able to put names with the cars." At the sixteenth annual event in 2002 staged in Irvine, California, Strauss had 2,100 paid attendees. They filled a 350-room Hyatt Hotel and overflowed into hotels and the homes of friends for miles around.

In between the design-and-production process and the buying-and-collecting hobby is Toy Fair. For nearly a decade, preparing the cars for Toy Fair and for television commercial and toy catalog photography was in the hands of Luis Montes de Oca in the samples department.

"While we were still at the old building," Montes de Oca explained, "we did a lot of presentations for our sales people and even for outside buyers in the turntable room. The marketing people would do their presentations, product names, advertising strategy, marketing plans, and then we'd turn everything around to show the buyers the toys and sets, tracks and everything."

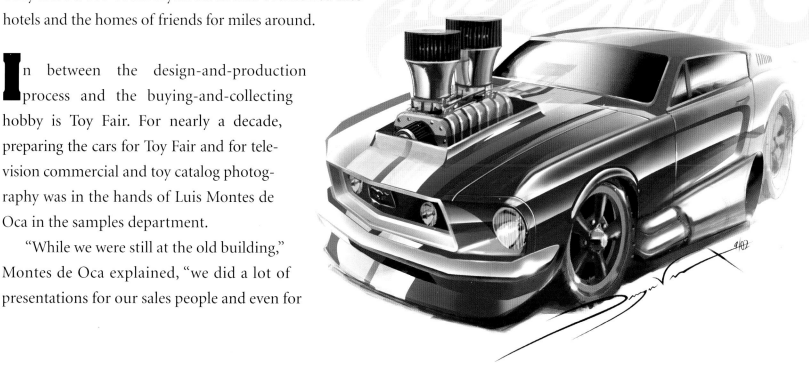

Mattel introduced its first Quad-Runner in 1987. This Suzuki QuadRacer appeared in pink, white, and yellow. As with all Hot Wheels cars at the time, model makers produced the original master block mold and then the shell molds in a mix of epoxy (the dark grey material) and resin (tan). This master, also typical of the period, is four-times the size of the Hot Wheels production version.

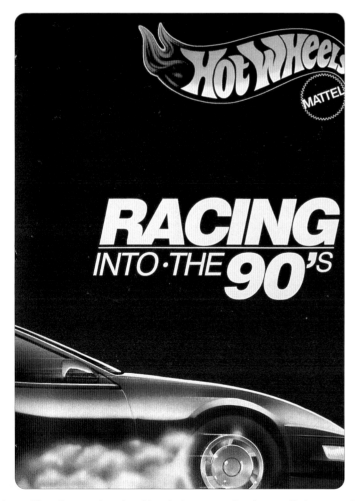

Mattel raced into the new decade with a dealer toy catalog that swelled to more than 100 pages. Among the Hot Wheels vehicles introduced in 1990 was the first without any wheels, the Propper Chopper helicopter.

Mattel used to throw its own Toy Fair, as well as a pre-Toy Fair. The company displayed preliminary toys that were close to a production start, and it occasionally took orders. The pre-Toy Fair was held a couple months before the Toy Fair to get an idea of what the buyers liked.

"The showroom was inside the huge ballroom. They'd hire contractors and construct cities inside the room. For Hot Wheels, we always did a race set that filled an entire ballroom. The engineers would spend weeks designing and testing it, then an entire week installing and constructing the sets. We'd do the shows, then tear everything down, pack it up, and ship it back. Toy Fair was like the World Series of Toys.

"Mattel would spend millions of dollars on each of these shows. They'd fly in all the buyers from all the big stores. Beautiful female models would show off the Hot Wheels and other boys' toys. Handsome male models would demonstrate Barbie and the other girls' toys."

The samples department was within Marketing, and Montes de Oca worked with ten to fifteen other people. Each person was a specialist in their line, although Marketing demanded they all know a bit about each other's products and be able to answer a question about any product. The samples department also shipped samples to regional presentations.

"The toys would go from designers to the model makers and after they'd finished producing the prototypes, we had them paint the cars as well," Montes de Oca said. "Then we would need to show them. Usually we got six or seven samples of each new toy. We got them to presentation. One marketing team might be in Dallas, and an opportunity to show the cars would come up in Chicago for Sears. Those handmade models usually cost a few thousand dollars each to make." Some smaller prototypes, such as Hot Wheels cars, were shipped by overnight express services. Other larger scale or more valuable toys were carried by Montes de Oca.

"One year we had a 1/8th scale radio-control, off-road truck. We had shown it at Toy Fair in New York. I flew out with it and I was to fly it home as my carry-on. I got bumped from the flight out of La Guardia. I had some time to kill so I started to play

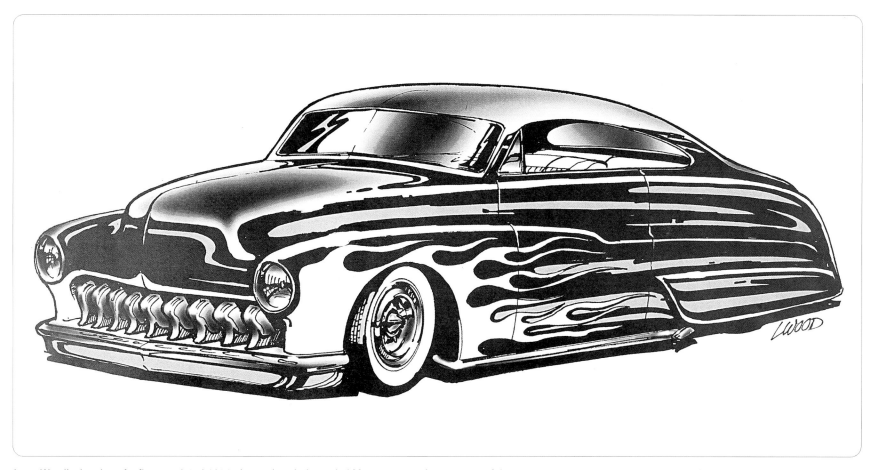

Larry Wood's drawing of a flame-painted 1951 chopped-and-channeled Mercury coupe became one of the most popular modern Hot Wheels cars. Called the Purple Passion, Mattel introduced it in 1990. A green version was released in 1995 as the Mean Green Passion.

with the truck, running it around the concourse. It had really been souped up so it was extremely fast. In fact, it ran so fast, I lost it. It ran out of range and coasted somewhere. I couldn't find it. I started running all over the airport. This thing cost $50,000 and there was only this one."

Montes de Oca soon found the car surrounded by airport security and a few startled passengers who had seen it come streaking toward them before getting stuck under a bench. After they finished lecturing him about airport security, they asked him about the toy and then told him to remove the batteries and not run it anymore.

Mattel had been producing Hot Wheels cars in France for the European market, but discontinued production there in 1986 because the facility in Penang, Malaysia, was more effective. A year later, production in Mexico ended, and that also moved to Penang. Outside Mattel, Strauss published his first price guide. It became obsolete almost immediately as the effect

of registering prices in print sparked a big jump in values. It struck some hobbyists and a few Wall Street observers who suffered from the market crash of October 19, 1987, that investing in Hot Wheels cars would have been much safer and more fun.

For the twentieth anniversary of Hot Wheels cars in 1988, under the leadership of new Mattel CEO John Amerman, who believed that the long-lived staples (Barbie, See 'N Say, and Hot Wheels) were underappreciated and undersold, the company celebrated the die-cast cars' heritage with a set of collector's edition models in chrome and gold chrome. It was a spectacular vacu-metallized finish that outshone the earliest Spectraflame models.

By 1989, with hundreds of employees laid off or shuffled to other departments, Luis Montes de Oca was transferred to Hot Wheels engineering. In those days, he and designers like Larry Wood and Michael Kollins designed one new body style and created new color schemes for one other car each month.

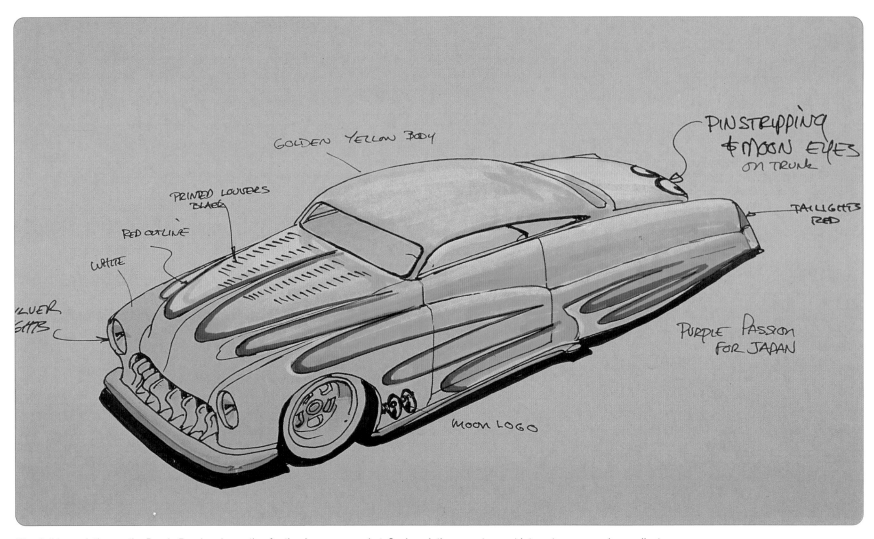

Wood did a variation on the Purple Passion decoration for the Japanese market. Such variations create great interest among serious collectors.

A variety of Sto & Go carrying case/play sets appeared in 1989. These were smaller than the original series and were restricted to a single level of vehicle travel. Still, the purpose was the same: to allow Hot Wheels owners to imagine themselves and their vehicles in adult working situations. The Firefighter, Service Station, and Building Site sets all involved new or existing Hot Wheels models in play situations.

For budding urban planners, Mattel proposed in 1991 that children might combine a number of its Hot Wheels City sets into one major metropolitan area. For those with imagination, track placement could simulate traffic control, with side streets forced to jump the edges of the free-flowing vehicle movement on major arteries.

"You had to get approval," Montes de Oca recalled, "of marketing, of legal, design, engineering, for the chassis and the body. Then came the handmade models and the rubdowns of the pad prints. I used to do all those by hand on the prototypes. It was very complicated. The cars were just 1/64th scale, so the tampos were very small. It was easy to be off a little bit, or if they didn't come out just right, you started over again.

"When we started doing all those racing cars, it was very complex. Michael Kollins had to keep files on all the cars. He had to get permissions for the decals and the names, and it wasn't for just one or two cars. We were doing fifteen, twenty, all different. It was amazing because more than half the cars were never produced because we couldn't get approval, or somebody wanted too much money to do the car. Sometimes that's what happened between the catalogs and the stores. Mattel would just pull the plug because it was impossible to get it approved."

The Hot Wheels design team was branching out into new areas, moving beyond designers' visions of custom cars and beginning to replicate real cars in Hot Wheels scale. This growth spurred the creation of an entire department to secure and manage the licensing rights for the Hot Wheels versions of actual cars produced by manufacturers around the world.

The year 1990 meant many things to Mattel and Hot Wheels cars. For one, a new licensing agreement put Hot Wheels cereal on grocery shelves. More significant was the growing awareness along Mattel's Mahogany Row of executive offices that the company's heritage offered some significant marketing, promotion, and sales growth opportunities. For Barbie, this meant the introduction of $30 and $120 collector's editions, the latter wearing a designer gown created by Hollywood legend Bob Mackie. For Hot Wheels cars, with the popularity of its twentieth anniversary sets, it meant new series, such as the California Customs, which reminded Mattel long-timers of Elliot's first references to Harry Bradley's wildly styled El Camino pickup truck that became the 1968 model Fleetside and launched the look of the entire line. Mattel had begun to enjoy a beneficial relationship with Disney in a new brand of preschool toys. This encouraged Mattel to strike a deal with 20th Century Fox. These licensing and marketing agreements developed

Larry Wood created the Speed Shark as a concept race car based on the predatory fish. It was produced in 1991.

and marketed products based on *The Simpsons* television series. In one of his last tasks before he left Mattel, Bob Rosas resurrected the Scene Machine technology and applied it to Homer Simpson's Nuclear Waste Van, which was introduced in 1990. It was widely known throughout Mattel that chairman John Amerman was a fan of the show.

Amerman made moves to insert more Mattel product, especially Hot Wheels cars, into the European marketplace. "There are more kinds of die casts in Western Europe alone than there are in the U.S. today," he told *Los Angeles Times* business writer John Evans Frook. "One day we'll be bigger there than here." To that end, the plant in Penang launched the first casting distributed exclusively outside of the United States.

Mattel made other moves in 1990, including a corporate and design relocation from the older six-story structure in Hawthorne to a new fifteen-story $36 million office tower in El Segundo not far from Los Angeles International Airport. The new design center, which housed girls' toys, boys' toys, and preschool toys, moved into an additional structure just a block away.

Recalling Mattel's first Hot Wheels fast food tie-in years before, Hot Wheels and Barbie both enjoyed great success as part of McDonald's Happy Meal promotions that began in 1991.

Ideal for any mall, especially if strategically placed close to a cash machine, the Hot Wheels vending machine concept was conceived by Mattel in the early 1990s.

Additional promotional tie-ins flourished, and each stressed the longtime appeal of Hot Wheels die-cast cars. Mattel created a new Hot Wheels cartoon series and a videotape collection of shows that was packaged with a special car and available by Christmas.

Early that year, designer Larry Wood called fellow Hot Wheels designer and good friend Steve Pennington. Pennington had started in the Hot Wheels model shop in 1966 at age eighteen and was among the first and youngest to become involved in the creation, development, and production of Hot Wheels cars. Pennington remained there until 1973 when the financial stresses of the company were hard to take. He went to nearby Revell and one of his first projects was to make a plastic kit of the Goodyear blimp. Pennington only stayed there six months, but his blimp went on to become one of Revell's best-selling kits. Wood asked if Pennington still had his drawings of the airship.

To emphasize the importance of Hot Wheels cars and allied marketing efforts to its customers, Mattel used this Trans-Am racing action photograph as the cover illustration for its 1993 toy catalog.

Mattel introduced the Pro Circuit Hot Wheels cars in 1992. This series of racing cars challenged both designers and Mattel's legal department. Not only did they each get team colors and sponsor decals depicted accurately, they had to obtain permission from each group as well. Ultimately this meant that several cars and teams went unrepresented. Cruz Pendregon's Funny Car and Scott Pruett's Champ car made it into production. Both the Maxwell House Coffee and the Interstate Battery NASCAR models were held up.

This is a paint and tampo test that Bob Rosas supervised on a collection of Pontiacs. The red '80s Firebird shows the paint and tampo combination that Mattel used to introduce the car for 1983. The blue Hot Bird, introduced in 1978, shows off a much simpler flame logo on its hood. The vacu-metallized gold Firebird Funny Car originally arrived in several colors as a 1982 model. It appeared in this gold in a Hot Wheels twentieth-anniversary set offered in 1988.

After Mattel introduced a helicopter in the 1990 lineup and had great success, it now added the Goodyear blimp for 1992. Wood added a rotating signboard feature that changed messages along the side of the blimp by twisting the tail section. In addition, Mattel introduced a new metalflake paint treatment, best known for its large metallic flakes within the color. Another lineup called the Gleam Team fitted a textured or wildly colored plastic body mounted onto a metal chassis and included such models as the Aeroflash concept car, the '56 Flashsider pickup truck, and the Flashfire, a concept sports car. The Pro Circuit line offered collectors a series of the more popular racing cars.

Matchbox began to produce cars in Macau in 1983, and it acquired the Dinky Toy line in 1987. Through the late 1980s, owner David Yeh had followed the Mattel toy philosophy and expanded into dolls, most notably a Pee-Wee Herman doll and a Freddy

Krueger talking doll from the *Nightmare on Elm Street* films. It was too much of an expansion, and in May 1992, Tyco Toys, the third largest toy company in the United States, acquired Matchbox. While Mattel had been interested in them back when Yeh acquired it, this time the company stayed out of the market.

The twenty-fifth anniversary of Hot Wheels cars in 1993 saw all-out celebrations when mega-retailer Toys 'R' Us commissioned its own exclusive commemorative line. Mattel retooled and reissued eight of the original 1968 models and packaged them in blister cards. The factory in Penang tampo-printed redlines on the tires and Mattel inserted plastic buttons reminiscent of the early metal badges in each package. With the creation of this lineup, chairman John Amerman followed through on his commitment to Mattel's core brands and placed another bet on the company's future by celebrating its past.

11

THE DEDICATION OF FOLLOWERS

Mattel expanded and extended the twenty-fifth anniversary commemoratives with a new Vintage Collection that was launched in 1994. The corporation appealed directly to collectors and received an enthusiastic response that few but the savviest observers anticipated. Knowing that major retailers Toys 'R' Us, Kmart, Wal-Mart, and others restocked their shelves overnight, the most serious collectors who recognized a new source of revenue for themselves developed wily techniques to get what they wanted. At the same time, they hoped certain others did not get these pieces.

A collector who lives in England recounted an example of the length to which collectors will go to secure Hot Wheels. From his view across the Atlantic, he's seen some interesting cars and observed some curious behaviors. "I know a chap called Fred, he's a proper dealer now, a distributor. Fred doesn't deal in secondhand stuff at all. When he was actively buying and selling that way, he operated with a friend who worked the morning shift at Boeing Aircraft. Fred would visit all the local stores. He and his friends had devised prearranged spots where Fred would hide stuff. One of the big delays in getting 'round to each of the big stores in the mornings is the long checkout lines. So Fred would see the good stuff when it came out, grab it, hide it somewhere, normally above the racks there, or stow it underneath. Between the towels in the linens department used to be a good one as well.

"His friend Pat would come by at three o'clock in the afternoon after the end of his work shift. The store would be relatively deserted and Pat would pull the packages out, take them up to checkout, and pay for it, calmly waiting in whatever line there might be. It was the system they devised to save time while getting to as many of the shops as possible. And that was their goal whenever Mattel introduced a new model, to hit as many shops as they could. The only way to succeed was not to be delayed at the checkout."

The question facing any of these collectors was if the cars they had purchased were going to be collectible. The variations that appeared as one model line finished off the last paint of another model are the most desirable to the serious collectors. One strategy to find out what schemes are collectible is to buy them all and sit on them for a month until the next run of the cars came out. If the pegs were refilled with purple cars with blue interiors, the buyers would return those and sit on the red ones until a collector convention happened, or until the advent of eBay and Internet shopping.

The gamble of distribution that sends red cars with yellow interiors to New England and purple cars with blue interiors to Southern California adds to the frenzy. With the advent of Internet selling systems, trash can quickly become a collector's treasure. Mattel recognized that and began its very popular Collector Series. It issues known quantities of cars in packaging that identifies the cars with a name and collector number.

When Mattel moved into its new office tower, it opened a company store on the ground floor just off the visitor parking lot. For Hot Wheels collectors in Southern California, it became a must-visit stop on their morning rounds. In the first year, the store manager placed the Hot Wheels sales racks inside the front door in easy view of front windows. The most serious buyers rolled through the parking lot just after first light of day to see if anything new had reached the shelves overnight. For the most part, they knew what was new because they had driven through the day before, and the day before that.

In the late fall of 1994, a collector visiting Hot Wheels design met Luis Montes de Oca. As they compared stories of the pranks

Starting in the early 1990s, Larry Wood began to create a Christmas gift car-and-blisterpack for his colleagues in Mattel's Design Center and for special friends outside the corporation. Continuing to this day, Wood takes regular production models and gives them custom paint colors and special decoration to commemorate the year and the holidays. These very special season's greetings are strictly limited in production and highly cherished by recipients.

that routinely occurred within the Hot Wheels collector world and inside Mattel's design center, the collector wondered aloud if they'd ever done an April Fool's Day issue, perhaps an invisible car?

The wheels started turning in Montes de Oca's head, and he went to Larry Wood, Michael Kollins, and a friend named Glenn in reprographics who had great computer design skills, to tell them what he had in mind.

Wood asked Montes de Oca what he was talking about, but Wood knew Montes de Oca and his humor. Wood is a brilliant designer with a quick and exceptional imagination. He's also, by his own admission, organizationally challenged. After he and the rest of the design staff moved into their new offices, his cubicle quickly became known as the Bermuda Triangle. Things went in, but they never came out.

Montes de Oca still wanted to create an invisible car. He took two blister cards and redesigned them with a friend in graphic

By 1996, when this Rail Rodder appeared with other toys such as the Goodyear Blimp and the Hydroplane in the Hot Wheels lineup, interesting vehicles were the primary requirement. No longer did every Hot Wheels vehicle have to handle banked turns or loops. This opened possibilities for Mattel's creative designers to do hot-rod locomotives and other curiosities. Dave Jones produced this perfectly detailed white resin prototype model.

While Mattel had produced faithful representations of Caterpillar's wheel loaders, forklifts, bulldozers, and other machines, this more fanciful creation is known as Street Cleaver. Mattel introduced this Larry Wood design in 1996. The rear blade flipped straight up to serve as an aerodynamic rear wing when not pushing or grading dirt. This is another white resin model by model maker Dave Jones.

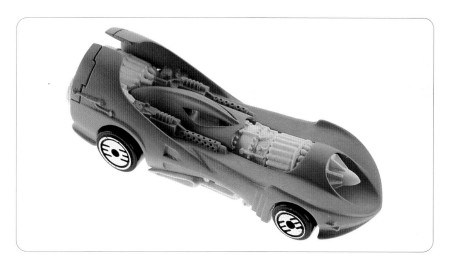

The classic Larry Wood-designed Jet Threat has moved in and out of the Hot Wheels product lineup under various names since the model was first introduced in 1971. This gray epoxy and white resin model shows how it re-emerged in 1995 as the Power Rocket, and again as the X-Ploder in 1999.

To better determine how the internal parts fit together, Mattel's model department produced a few clear-bodied Power Rocket models.

The Road Rocket was introduced as a 1996 First Editions model. In each subsequent year, Hot Wheels designers modified the body color and decoration, leading to this 2002 version, the Subterranean Recovery Crew, in gold chrome and plastic. This reflects a Mattel practice from the earliest days: Introduce a toy, change its appearance, modify its decoration, and reintroduce it every year or two for as long as interest remains.

Mattel introduced the Ford Escort Rally Car as #1 in its 1998 First Editions series. It appeared then as a white rally-race car, and it reappeared a year later as a black City of Hot Wheels police car in the Police Squad Pack. It returned to its race-car roots in 2002.

arts. The toy number was 0000 and the collector number was 000. They named the car the "Invisible Car" and gave it a fake UPC code on the back so it wouldn't accidentally be sold.

"Then I got some wheels and axles and I hot-glued them to the blister so they wouldn't roll around or fall. I finished this on Saturday. April Fool's that year was on a Sunday, and I took them to the company store that afternoon. I had a key and I hid

them on the rack inside the other Hot Wheels so they would be ready when the store opened Monday, and I closed up and left."

Around 2 P.M. on Monday afternoon, Maria from the company store called Montes de Oca.

"We have a problem here," she told him. She did not sound happy. "All the collectors have raided the pegs and there's a collector here who has found an invisible car."

Mattel introduced the Rodger Dodger in 1974 as a hot-rodded version of Dodge's early 1970s Charger muscle car. Larry Wood played with the car's shape and decoration to produce the model. In 1976, Mattel brought the car back as part of the Super Chromes lineup. It reappeared in all chrome in 1998 as part of a Hot Wheels 30th Anniversary promotion.

Mattel introduced the Jeepster concept vehicle as a 1999 First Editions model. For 2000, Mattel produced a large run for the Philadelphia Phillies with the teams logo printed on the hood as game promotional giveaways. This green version appeared in 2001.

This Hot Wheels Racing open-wheel racer was one of many designs that Mattel did for McDonald's. The basic car appeared first as the 1999 Grand Prix selection. The same car was offered in red as a Ferrari, yellow as a Jordan, black as a McLaren, white as a Stewart, and red or blue with white as a Williams. Each version was appropriately decorated with racing decals and numbers. This undecorated green version was a McDonald's premium in 2000.

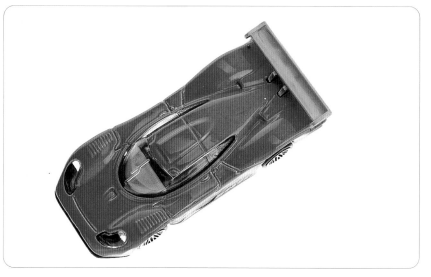

Soon after Porsche brought its full-size model to the automotive world, the Hot Wheels version Porsche 911 GT-198 first hit the shelves in 1999. In a variation offered later in the year, Hot Wheels designers decorated the car as it looked while winning the 24 Hours of Le Mans race. For 2002, Mattel redecorated the car in this orange metalflake paint finish with Hot Wheels logos on the sides. In recent years, Mattel has offered significant racing cars looking as they did when they made their history. These appeal to race-car collectors in addition to children and other adult collectors.

"I thought, 'Uh-oh,' but I said, 'What in the world are you talking about?'"

"There's a guy here who is trying to pay for a car that won't run through the computer. The UPC code on the back is not registering, and it's a big mess." Montes de Oca grabbed Wood and they went over to the store.

When they got there, it was a big mess. Hot Wheels blister cards were strewn all over the floor. The collectors saw the two invisible cars and went everywhere looking for more.

"How many of these invisible cars are there?" Maria asked.

"To tell you the truth, I don't know. You can't see them." Maria didn't laugh.

DC in CLEAR
LIGHT
DRIFTWOOD

One of the most popular recent models is this Customized VW Drag Bus, introduced by Mattel in 1996. It has reappeared frequently in a wide variety of paints and decorations. Hot Wheels Convention founder Mike Strauss produced a limited run in green as the formal dinner gift to convention attendees in 2002.

Mattel designers often create cars in their program called Plausible Original Designs. Under this heading, the designer gets to imagine what the next generation of a car might look like if they were to design it. One designer contemplated what the next generation Chevrolet Camaro might look like. Mattel called this Muscle Tone and introduced it in 2000. This is one of the color combinations for 2001.

First introduced in 2001, the Hyper Mite was redecorated as the Hot Wheels Extreme City Police cruiser in 2002.

Hot Wheels designers alternate between adopting full-size cars that people can own, fantasy concept vehicles that adults can only wish they might have, and full-size vehicles that car enthusiasts in the United States have heard about but cannot import. Such is this Lotus Elise model 340R, a highly desirable high-performance English sports car not yet available to buyers in the U.S. Mattel introduced its car in 2000.

Monoposto is the Italian word for "single seater," which describes this racer concept car introduced in 2001 as the Monoposto. It first appeared as #19 in the 2001 First Editions series.

Mattel first released the Dodge concept pickup truck Sidewinder in 1998. It appeared in the 1998 First Editions series as #3, and then Mattel reissued the convertible truck in this maroon paint in the Company Car series.

The Shredster first appeared in red with dark yellow fenders as #10 in the 2001 First Editions series. This yellow body with black fenders is a variation from that year.

"I'm going to ask you again. How many invisible cars did you make?"

"I made two."

"Is that it?"

"So far as I know."

"Okay, well where's the other one?" Montes de Oca had no answer for this question.

There was a customer in her office with one blister pack. He wouldn't let go. Maria had explained that without a UPC, she didn't know what to charge for it. He said he'd pay anything they wanted.

Wood and Montes de Oca escaped quickly, and left Maria to sort out what had happened. Montes de Oca was afraid he was in trouble because of the mess on the floor of the store. Wood

Larry Wood designed this dry lake speed-record coupe in 2001. The Sooo Fast has received several decorations since then, including one as a classic flamed-out hot rod similar to Wood's original concept.

The Ford F-150 pickup truck is America's best selling truck, and Mattel has redecorated this model, first released in 1997, through countless variations, including two versions of this flame paint. It first incorporated the Harley-Davidson motorcycle logo on the doors and hood in 2001. This alternate appeared only as part of the Wreck 'N' Roll track set in 2001.

XS-IVE is a fire fighter/rescue concept truck. It appeared as vehicle #28 in the 2001 First Editions series, in red, yellow, and black. In 2002, it showed up in this guise as the Missle Range Retrieval Vehicle.

Mattel introduced its replica of the Honda Spocket show car in 2002. This compact, cab-forward pickup truck concept vehicle earned Honda a great deal of coverage when the full-size car was revealed in 2001.

This 2002 model is the Open Road-ster, a concept sports car/racer with a chrome engine and a big spoiler on the back. It first appeared as #21 in the 2002 First Editions series.

This concept racer is called HW Prototype 12. This model, introduced in 2002, led more than a few car-design enthusiasts and Hot Wheels collectors to wonder what the other 11 prototypes might have looked like.

Sometimes known as Shadow Jet II and otherwise called the Stealth, this car first appeared in 1994. In this decoration from late 2002, it was #5 of the Fire Crew set. It demonstrates a revised Hot Wheels philosophy that previously did not allow designer's to create cars that looked fascinating yet could not negotiate tight banked turns or loops.

asked him repeatedly if there was really only one card. Montes de Oca had no idea what happened to the other, but figured someone recognized what it was, found only one, and stole it.

"I never found out what Maria did about that guy, or what happened to the other invisible car, but that was supposed to be the end of the story. But then in the daily Hot Wheels meeting, all the Hot Wheels people knew about it.

"You know, Luis, this is the best thing we ever did for Mattel. Let's just make Invisible Cars. There's no tooling involved

and people will happily pay us ten dollars for each one. And think about doing limited editions. And what about the variations that collectors love, we could *tell* them one of them had a special interior."

Despite such controversial cost-saving approaches as invisible cars, Hot Wheels visible cars did very well from 1995 on. That was because marketing put a laser focus on the foundation of the business: cars, track, and play sets. As Jim Wagner,

In the Plausible Original Design program, Hot Wheel designers update full-size cars as they might look if Hot Wheels designers redid them. This is one designer's vision of the legendary Ford GT40 racer, the 40-Somethin'.

One of the design heroes of Hot Wheels' design chief is former auto designer, now futurist artist, Syd Mead. Mead's ideas and philosophy formed the basis for this Sentinel 400 Limo. The spectacularly stretched, lowered, chopped, and channeled luxury car first appeared in 2002.

Michael Kollins works at the computer in his office space surrounded by the hundreds of cars he has been involved with. The Hot Wheels gas station, at right rear, a 1950s replica, houses a conference room and private offices.

THE HOT WHEELS DESIGN CENTER

The Design Center at Mattel's El Segundo facility is like Willy Wonka's Chocolate Factory for car enthusiasts: filled with tempting delights from three-and-a half decades of ingenuity and creativity. In addition to the highly skilled individuals filling the cubicles, Mattel has invested in state-of-the-art technology for its design staff: CAD systems, stereo lithography, and laser scanning. These machines in no way replace the skill and creativity of designers, but like any great tool they amplify that creative ability by allowing the creator to execute his or her vision with more efficiency. This results in some of the most exciting and best produced die-cast toys ever created.

This rare, behind-the-scenes look at the Design Center is enough to make even the most casual Hot Wheels collector giddy with excitement. . . .

160

A Hot Wheels senior designer, puts the finishing touches on his renderings of the Pony-Up, his interpretation of the next generation of Ford Mustang. Designers use B-sheets, 11x17-inch vellum paper, as well as computer pads to create their cars.

Hot Wheels designers have a broad palette of colors to chose from when designing a car. And in case they forget, an enclosed case displays models in every paint variation possible, along with the identification codes for each hue.

2001 . 2002 . 2003 FIRST EDITIONS

"Graphic Designer's" Vehicle Reference - Please return after referencing.

Graphic artists now decorate the cars on computer screen. When Product Planning calls for new graphics on a recently introduced model, the artist can rescan these video-friendly blue models and design directly on their computer.

The top layers of workspace certainly offer a kind of candy-store visual temptation, with production models mingling with prototypes. This is the top of Larry Wood's office area.

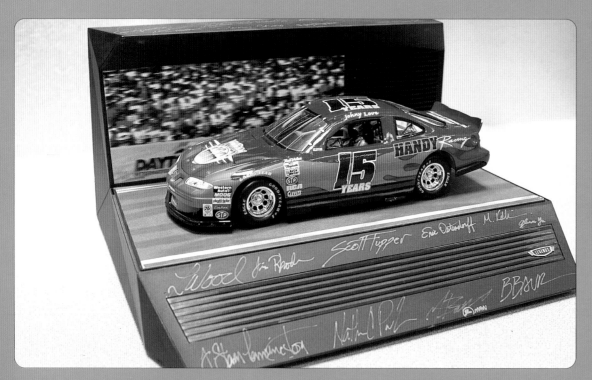

Many companies reward longtime employees with watches. The Hot Wheels design staff does its own thing, customizing existing or prototype models with special paint and decoration. In this instance they honor Senior Vice President of Design, John Handy, for his fifteen years with the company.

Their own history on display, design staff walk past four packed showcases of Hot Wheels history many times a day. Staffers know these showcases, and often their design cubicles are filled with models that would make serious collectors weak in the knees.

Children can battle against a giant octopus with the Octoblast track set.

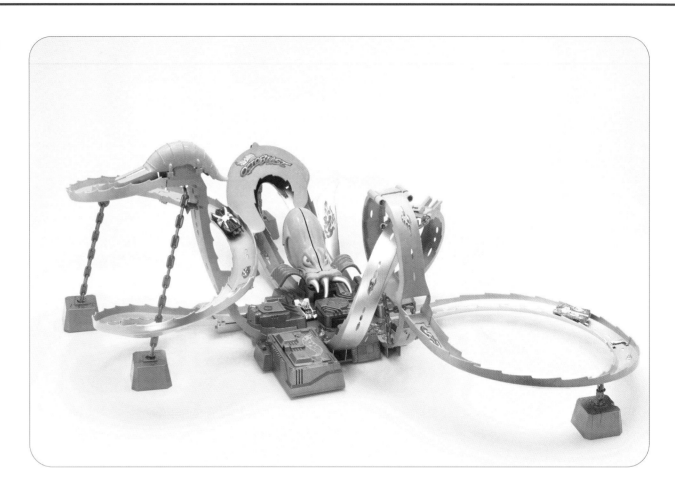

senior vice-president of marketing, put it, "we really spent time and effort reexamining the design of the cars, the track sets, and the performance of the cars on the track sets."

Mattel focused on one segment per year. The first focus was the cars, and the track and play sets followed. Wagner said these core toys are evergreen because they allow children to take on new challenges, face risks, and ultimately prove themselves.

"When I was a kid, I took my Hot Wheels cars, went down a way-too-steep ramp, through the loop, and if they made the jump and stayed on the track, it was a big accomplishment. That was a way to challenge myself as a child. Boys today still challenge themselves with track sets. For example, we have one called Octoblast, where cars battle a giant octopus. From a kid's perspective, it's great, because this car-eating giant animal is challenging me. And I can defeat it."

Wagner's words reflect a return to Elliot Handler's two fundamental themes: take a little device, find more and more ways to use it, and make sure it has play value so that the children participate in the play activities. In 1968, it was making the car do the loop. Now,

Is this a reasonable product marketing tie-in, or a very clever way to keep youngsters hard at work with pencils ever-sharp? This Hot Wheels pencil sharpener appeared with the muscle car concept Overbored 454. Other cars were available as well in 2002.

thirty-five years later, the challenge is more metaphysical, more grandiose of purpose, such as battling a giant octopus. It is as if Wagner and Amerman had ascribed to Joseph Campbell's concept of the hero's journey. Perhaps to some extent, grander purposes of active play are necessary in order to keep eight- and nine-year-olds

This concept from the Plausible Original Design program is called Overbored 454. It represents Mattel's thinking about what the next Chevrolet Chevelle might look like if it were still in production. The Overbored 454 first appeared in 2002 as #16 in the 2002 First Editions series.

The Hyper Liner concept mini-van is a convertible vehicle, offering additional play value. With the slide of a lever on the chassis, the yellow van body comes off to reveal an ultra-low-riding, roll-caged four-passenger open-air cruiser. It is reminiscent of beach and dune buggies but with low ground clearance for use on the pavement.

The Dragon Wagon was first introduced in 1993, and it returned in a variety of decorations in 1995 as the Speed Blaster. Mattel later packaged the car as part of a Tony Hawk Skate series, with the name "Birdhouse" printed on the nose.

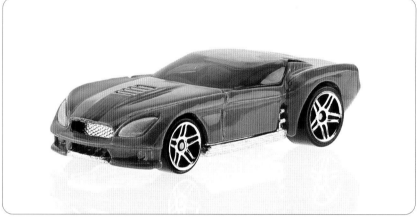

Pony-Up was a senior project designer's vision of what the next Mustang might look like. A former Ford car designer, he saw Ford acquire English sports-car maker Aston Martin and recognized that the Aston is one of the world's most desirable cars. His concept incorporates the swelled fenders and tapered cockpit cues from the $200,000 Aston and offers them in what might be a $25,000 Mustang.

on the floor with their toy cars instead of retiring to the television to battle cyber morphs.

Looking at Hot Wheels cars, one simple view is that they are toys and while kids grow older at a younger age these days, there is a new crop of children born every year. American and world business can't survive without growth, and letting the audience outgrow the product is not acceptable.

"We've really done a lot of research in order to find out what Hot Wheels means to consumers," Wagner continued. "We found most recently that boys don't stop liking Hot Wheels cars as they grow older, and they don't lose their emotional tie to the brand. We had just stopped giving them products that were relevant to them.

"For instance, one of the hottest trends right now is action sports. One way that Mattel continues to encourage children to challenge themselves is through our action sports products. We now have Hot Wheels licensed skateboards and BMX performance bikes. If you're going to do a cool stunt or a great trick on a bike or a skateboard, you can do it on a Hot Wheels version."

Here the Sling Shot concept sports/race car wears Hot Wheels Highway 35 logos commemorating the 35th anniversary of Hot Wheels cars in 2003. As part of the 35th anniversary celebration, Mattel has reintroduced collector badges in cardboard, similar to what was offered in the late 1960s and early 1970s.

This is the spectacular result of the partnership between Ferrari and Mattel.

Moto-Crossed, first introduced in 2002, was part of the Roadbeasts series for the World Race promotion surrounding the Hot Wheels 35th anniversary celebration. As a cross between a concept off-roader and a conceptualized moto-cross quad-runner, this design is as radical and innovative as anything an enthusiast might see at an international auto show.

To maintain the association of cool with Hot Wheels for older boys worldwide, Mattel launched a program called Authentication Through Association to make the Hot Wheels brand come to life. The company looked at the aspects that appeal to car enthusiasts on a global basis. This led to Mattel's association with NASCAR, the world's fastest growing spectator sport. To align itself with the sport, they negotiated a sponsorship with NASCAR legend Kyle Petty.

According to Wagner, linking Hot Wheels with a leading name in NASCAR was only the beginning. "The next opportunity that attracted us was the whole action sports genre, and we knew we could not be as bold and as blatant. So we found sports where Hot Wheels seemed relevant. We did it with Tony Hawk, and just like with Kyle's career, we were fortunate enough to be Tony's sponsor when he did the 900, which many feel was the most dramatic event in action sports history.

"We were there with Jeremy McGrath when he won some of his world championships. We've been with Tony Parker when he did great things in the X-Games. The result is that Hot Wheels was put in front of car enthusiasts and action sports fans wherever they went: at the Detroit Auto Show, at NASCAR events, at the X-Games. The next step was to grow the brand internationally."

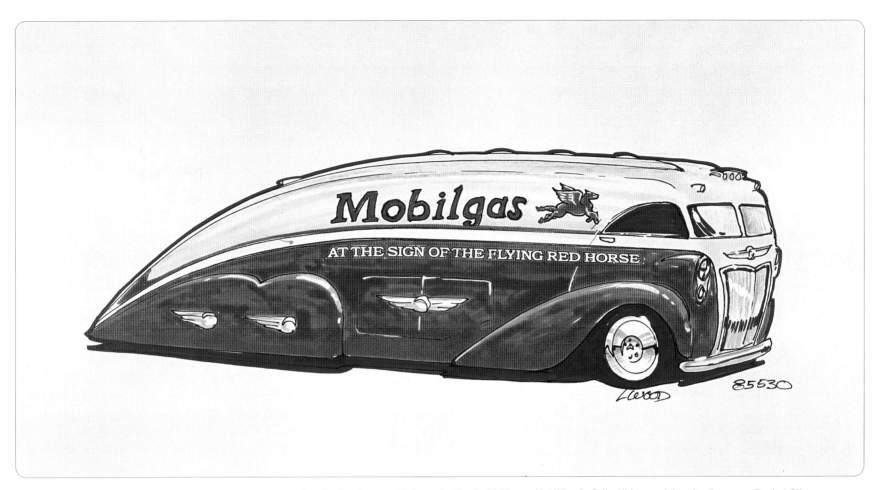

First conceived as a retro-styled fuel tanker from the 1930s, Wood's drawing went into production in 2000 as a Hot Wheels Collectibles model under the name Rocket Oil.

Larry Wood named this project the Elwoody, and it first appeared in a Hot Wheels Collectibles two-pack labeled Elwoody Custom Cars. This is Wood's interpretation of the 1950 Buick station wagon complete with a surfboard.

Don "The Snake" Prudhomme won many races in his Funny Car. This Legends to Life Hot Wheels car pays homage to Prudhomme and his racing career.

That direction led to Modena, Italy, home of Ferrari, the company with the fifth-most-recognized brand name in the world. Mattel decided it was time to enter the large scale business. After its successes with Petty, Hawk, McGrath, and Parker, being linked to number one was the only option. It was something of a quest, but Mattel walked in with the advantage of being the world's best known die-cast cars. While negotiations took time, Ferrari became a willing partner even as it contractually called on Mattel to produce its most famous cars in scale metal.

Model makers once produced master wood patterns for the tooling. They learned and polished their skills with the tutelage of men such as Del Paddock and Hal Krueger.

But model makers could see the handwriting on the wall. In the early 1980s, the Design department received its first computer-aided-design (CAD) system. It could generate models and patterns. Some model makers decided to "go over to the carpet"—leave the hard, wood-shaving-covered floor of the model shop for the soft, cushy life in Design.

One interesting task performed in the model shop was determing which model was the absolute fastest Hot Wheels car. This was a two-week long test. A track was built with a drop-off

and a flat run-out, and thousands of races with hundreds of cars were run. For one model maker this task sparked another idea altogether. In April 1998, several Hot Wheels designers set up a Hot Wheels racetrack at the Second Annual Winston Cup NASCAR Race at the new California Speedway. "The crowd had a great time racing Hot Wheels on this track, even with its poor design," one model maker recalled. Immediately after that event, he began the design and building of his new "Hot Wheels International Raceway."

Based on the previous track design, Larry Wood had already determined that weight would always win. During a racing match between staffers, Wood showed up with a 1-1/2-inch diameter solid steel ball with a painted Hot Wheels logo on it. It won every time. The track was redesigned to make sure the fastest vehicle won—not necessarily the heaviest. To accomplish that, the last ten feet of track became horizontal run-out. The flat run-out at the end of the track took care of the weight advantage—and now the fastest cars were winning.

A tranportable racetrack was devised, ten lanes wide and six feet high that allowed the cars to travel forty feet. At the end, cars zipped through a sensor-equipped finish line that mechanically determined the winner. One of Hot Wheels' engineering wizards created the finish line.

"Sounds easy? Not quite," laughed the track's designer. "Remember, a 1/64th-scale car free-rolling down a forty-foot

Here are some fabulous examples of 1/18th-scale Hot Wheels cars.

It's a tradition inside Mattel's design center that artists, designers, and engineers create a memorable gift when one of their own reaches a milestone employment anniversary. In 2001, in honor of Larry Wood's thirtieth year with the company, his colleagues created an animated scale model of the multi-talented designer in typical multi-tasking mode. As he drew a car with a marker on a B-sheet, he airbrushed a different rendering while beginning restoration of a challenged automobile. A tiny blender on his desk kept many balls in the air at the same time.

Beginning in 1997, Mattel sponsored a Hot Wheels stock car in the NASCAR Winston Cup series with driver Kyle Petty. *CIA Stock Photo, Inc.*

seamless track generates a scale speed of two hundred miles per hour as it crosses the finish line." The new track premiered at the Hot Wheels thirtieth anniversary convention in nearby Anaheim. Since then, dozens of weekends have been donated to hauling the track thousands of miles to give children and adults a chance to find out what model is the fastest Hot Wheels car. Which car is it? Mattel will never tell.

Perhaps Carson Lev can help answer that question. Lev joined Mattel in 1996 and worked on Disney Entertainment Group projects as he waited for a job to open up in the Hot Wheels section. While Lev was part of the Disney group, he heard of a Hot Wheels project to create a life-size, running model of Ira Gilford's 1969 Twin Mill car to show at the thirtieth anniversary celebration. As time passed, he learned it never had been completed. When the job opened for director of Design for Hot Wheels die-cast, Lev got the position.

The Twin Mill was, in everyone's estimation, the very first Mattel-designed Hot Wheels car. Harry Bradley's Deora first had been a Dodge show car, and the Custom Fleetside was inspired by Bradley's own everyday transportation. To Lev, the Twin Mill was the icon that represented Hot Wheels cars and Hot Wheels design. When Lev expressed this feeling to his new boss, John Handy, the senior vice-president of design, Handy turned the yet-to-be-completed project over to him.

Gilford's original concept for the car was all rear end. He envisioned the rear tires more as a single black cylinder, a tube. With that part of the design in place, he worked forward from there. When Gilford got to the front end, he had a vast amount of space available and decided to install two engines. While Gilford labeled it Dream I, Packaging's Carol Robinson invented the Twin Mill name, and the legend grew from there.

The full-size car first came to life under the direction of Boyd Coddington and his design director, Chip Foose. They created a chassis, acquired two supercharged 502-ci Chevy engines, and installed them along with the running gear. They designed and built a suspension and had begun to make the body when Coddington's business failed. Larry Wood and Lev managed to get the car out of Coddington's shop and over to Scott Tupper. The car sat in storage for a year.

Lev and Wood both knew Bob Larivee Sr. and Jr., and their Championship Auto Shows business. The Larivees struck a deal to split the cost to finish the car in exchange for show rights. Everyone agreed and they moved the project to Carron Industries, an outside fabricator that routinely did prototype work for Ford Motor Company. Carron finished the car completely, and Mattel unveiled it at the Specialty Equipment Marketing Association (SEMA) convention in 2001.

"When we presented the car," Lev explained, "we didn't want to just have a car in our booth with no relationship to what we do or who we are or why we did that car. Our goal at SEMA was to provide relevant products for adults in the form of automotive aftermarket and car-care products. To that end, we made mock-ups of licensed products, wheels, tires, bolt-on accessories, car wax, car wash products, and clothing. We made up a bunch of things just as props for the booth. The unveiling brought every local TV station and a few car specialty networks. Then everybody from wheel companies, paint companies, wax companies, clothing companies, and aftermarket accessory companies came to visit us. We got so much interest from real suppliers that we signed licensing deals right there at SEMA."

Mattel always thought that Hot Wheels cars appealed to men. It researched how many men had grown up and learned about cars through these toys. The total number was forty-one million, and these men still think of Hot Wheels cars as what a real car should be.

Some of the people who fit into that category have remarkable power to determine what real cars should be. After Sam Djujic retired from Mattel, he rewarded himself with a new Porsche Boxster. While he liked the car, he had some thoughts about its design. After months of making calls, he connected one day with Grant Larsen who worked at Porsche's Southern California design facility and had designed the Boxster.

"'You worked at Mattel?' Djujic remembered Grant asking him. "'You folks are responsible for me being an automobile designer. When you came out with Hot Wheels, I was a kid and I

Mattel's current state-of-the-art model-making process yields these intricately detailed one-to-one scale models made, in many cases, directly from scanned photographs or drawings. The models emerge from a vat filled with molten plastic.

While the interior decor of Hot Wheels design reflects the rose-colored recollections of the 1950s, its outside image is right up to date. Just turn on any computer and go to HotWheelsCollectors.com. Then hang on for a fast ride through information, history, questions and answers, sneak peeks at up-coming product, and chances to order merchandise produced in limited quantities. Serious collectors head to the website several times daily to find the latest.

Mattel launched the site in 2001, the brainchild of Amy Boylan, Mattel's senior vice-president, New Media. HotWheelCollectors.com now has more than 200,000 members, making it the largest die-cast collector "community" on the Internet. Membership gives participants access to the "Ask Hot Wheels" forum, a way to in-teract with other collectors and Hot Wheels staff. A partnership with eBay allows collectors to search every Hot Wheels auction without leaving HotWheelCollectors.com. There are series of vehicles available only to members. Mattel launched the four-teen-car HWC Series One in 2002 exclusively on the site. This series reintroduced red-line tires and Spectraflame-style paint on serial-numbered cars in a 10,000 model run.

Late in 2001, at the suggestion of collectors, HWC inaugu-rated a premium membership organization, called the Red Line Club. Mattel decided to limit membership in 2002 to just 15,000, and the club sold out within a week. For 2003, member-ship was capped at 18,000. Members received a Hot Wheels red-line replica; in 2002 it was the 1967 Camaro and for 2003 it was the 1968 Mustang. Access to some sections of the website are limited only to Red Line Club members.

According to Boylan, HotWheelsCollectors.com is "the sin-gle most effective way we have to get information—about new cars, new ideas, new personnel—out to our most loyal enthusiasts and customers, and to get information, feedback, reaction, and requests back from them. And all of it happens within a matter of minutes."

went Hot Wheels crazy. I had to have every model, every color. I became a car nut and I've stayed a car nut. I went to the Art Cen-ter of Design so I could make a living as a car nut. You guys are responsible for what I do. What did you do with Mattel?'" When Djujic answered his question, their conversation continued for another hour.

Car designers who work for the world's major auto companies love to visit the Hot Wheels design center. Along one wall, Lev, Wood, and Handy created a 1950s-era gas station complete with vintage pumps. Inevitably all visits end up inside the gas station where a small conference table is surrounded by shelf space that shows off the latest of the new Hot Wheels models introduced each year.

Outside the station on the oil racks, Lev encouraged all the de-signers to make their own oil can logos. Larry's Snake Oil is one of the many. The subtle and not-so-subtle sight gags make visitors laugh. The level of technology makes others in the automotive-design business sober because their own design studios have exactly the same equipment.

A program called Plausible Original Design, created by Hot Wheels design director was conceived to give Hot Wheels designers the freedom to think about what Detroit would do if

A strong fascination with tuner cars, the hot-rodded Japanese compacts that are stars in such films as *The Fast and the Furious* led to this Honda Civic, introduced in 2002.

The Hot Wheels version of the Ford Focus tuner car has a huge rear wing, fit for some twenty-first century drag racing. This car was first introduced in 2001, though this version appeared in 2002. New decorations honor Mattel's senior vice-president of the Boys Division, John Handy. Mattel's designers often put names familiar to them, friends, family, even household pets, on the graphics packages of their cars.

Mattel's Tunerz series features exaggerated tuner cars. This Toyota Supra, emblazened with Toyo Tires logos, first appeared in the series in 2002. While the Tunerz don't bear Hot Wheels logos, they are among the most popular new styles coming out of Mattel's design center.

TUNER CARS

When contemporary car culture evolved from dedication to devastatingly powerful car stereo to devastatingly powerful and stylishly modified compacts and imports, Mattel's youngest Hot Wheels designers, were right there. One young designer recalled that his first car was a 1978 Mustang with a huge stereo. By the time he graduated from college and joined the Hot Wheels design staff, he had moved on to a Mitsubishi Eclipse. When he got to Los Angeles, he really got into tuner stuff.

"The first car I designed for Hot Wheels was Sho-Stopper [introduced in 2000]. I didn't own my Eclipse yet, but I designed the Hot Wheels car as if I was going to own it." His original B-sheet drawing featured a red car, just like his own car is today. Designers keep up on all the latest trends in the tuner car world. "I read all the magazines, dozens of them, go to all the shows. I have friends who are drag racers, tuners, builders, kids in my neighborhood who build street racers, so I can see what they're doing. I take all that interest I've got and all the expertise I'm gathering and turn it toward the tuner cars we're doing. The Import Tuners, the kind of cartoon cars, that is my line. I've done all the cars in that line."

The goal with the Hot Wheels tuners line is to capture a new consumer by doing something more contemporary and focusing on the individuals who are buying cars today. The Import Tuners line's designer, who first joined Mattel as an intern in 1999 at the age of twenty-three, sticks to what real cars are interesting and accessible to him. "For a guy my age, to build a '32 Ford or an old Camaro is a daunting task. First, trying to find a decent car that is not too expensive and then to go through the cost of all the parts, I can't do that. But boy, I can take a good $3,000 to $5,000 Civic with a good body and build and build and build from paycheck to paycheck."

Sho-Stopper and the cars that followed in quick succession speak directly to that audience. In 2001, Mattel introduced its Honda Civic and the MS-T Suzuka. A Toyota Celica joined the 2001 lineup, followed in 2002 by the Custom Cougar, a tuner interpretation of the new generation Mercury Cougar; a Nissan Skyline; Super Tsunami, a tuner concept coupe; and Tantrum, a tuner concept roadster.

"The Import Tuners line is exploding at retail now. And it's understandable. All the big events for tuner cars are drawing larger and larger crowds. I travel to all the events in L.A., but I also go to the granddaddy of them all, the NOPI Nationals, the NOPI Parts sponsored show at Atlanta Motor Speedway. It's for everything from mini-trucks and SUVs to pickup trucks and import cars. Last year there were 6,000 cars and 100,000 people over two days. It's a huge show."

That makes for a huge audience for the latest Hot Wheels adventure.

Mattel designed the next generation of any production car. They had already created a new Ford GT40 that they called 40 Some-thin'. One Hot Wheels designer who had been at Ford before coming to Mattel, began thinking about a new Mustang in May 2001. "I knew that the Aston Martin Vantage was Ford Motor Company's most exotic, desirable sports car," He explained. "I adopted design cues to give a buyer the best features of the $200,000 exclusive English models in their $20,000-something Mustang. But what I did is much rounder, while Ford's concept is more angular." Hot Wheels marketing named his car Pony-Up. The little car did not go unnoticed.

When Ford's design vice-president, J. Mays, met with Hot Wheels staff at the November 2002 Specialty Equipment Mar-keting Association trade show in Las Vegas, he told John Handy and Carson Lev that, for the previous year or more, he sent his designers out to gather everything they could find that repre-sented Mustang. He wanted them to study what the car meant to customers, enthusiasts, and observers. Mays told Handy and Lev that during their search his designers found Pony-Up. He said, "There was more than one time that we returned to that model, because we found that it synthesized what we look at as a Mustang."

For Hot Wheels Design's youngest designer that concept of Plausible Original Designs is something near and dear. It landed him his full-time job. He was a second-time intern in Hot Wheels design at age twenty-three, and on break from studying industrial design. He designed two cars, ShoStopper (now called Seared Tuner) and Muscle Tone, the latter his tribute to the her-itage of the Camaro as a Generation Five Camaro. It was his first design that Mattel approved for production. Since he joined the company, he has seen two cars a year go into production, which is something his friends from school who went to Detroit envy.

"I live in a fantasy world, I tell you. If I'm designing a track set or a Hot Wheels car, or even when I'm doing a replica, I'm scaling down only the coolest cars. We don't make a four-door Taurus. We make a NASCAR Taurus, so we only make the cool stuff."

Growing up in Ohio, Hot Wheels' youngest designer was into mini-trucks. Now that he is in California, he has gotten involved with import tuner cars. He focuses on what is new and hip in the aftermarket for kids. He's taken what he's learned and turned it into the Hot Tunerz line.

"When I graduated, I thought about all the cars I liked, and all the cars I wanted to drive. And I realized that Detroit wasn't making any of them. And I'd heard they don't look too kindly on designers driving import cars there, no matter how cool they are. Now I'm working in a place where the only reason they care what I drive is to see if it could be a new car line for us. And I get to design the kinds of cars I'd like to drive."

As a part of the ongoing celebration called Hot Wheels Highway 35 to honor the thirty-fifth anniversary of The World's Coolest Car Company, Mattel unveiled a number of events and promotions. Few would dispute that title. Early in 2003, Hot Wheels history moved into a permanent space on the second floor of the Petersen Automotive Museum on fashion-able Wilshire Boulevard in Los Angeles. The result of more than five years of work, the large display shows off more than $200,000 worth of die-cast vehicles as well as six full-size cars representing what Hot Wheels are all about. At any given time, museum visitors can see the Twin Mill, the original Deora de-signed by Harry Bradley; two of Don "the Snake" Prudhomme's funny cars; Hot Wheels designer Scott Tupper's personal 1923 T-bucket roadster bedecked with Hot Wheels decals; the newest J. Mays/Ford Motor Company/Hot Wheels collaboration, the Hot Wheels edition Ford Focus; and museum founder Bob Petersen's 0032, a Chip Foose-designed streamlined hot rod. Three inter-active kiosks let visitors search for their favorite Hot Wheels die-cast car and learn how it and other models are manufac-tured. In addition, there is a large display of new large-scale models mounted on electro-luminescent shelves that seemingly surround the cars with light.

The large-scale model line, including 1/18th scale and 1/24th scale for NASCAR stock cars, has become a successful and signifi-cant part of the Hot Wheels appeal to collectors. A number of these models are exclusive to Mattel, specifically the entire Ferrari collection. In fact, when Ferrari introduced its recent 360 Modena,

Mattel co-launched its 1/18th-scale model of the car, prompting one magazine writer to observe that he'd only just driven the best car in his life and now he had it on his desk. In this vein, Chevrolet's much-awaited unveiling of the new Corvette C6 will go hand in hand with the release of the large-scale Hot Wheels collectible version. Other popular 1/18th-scale Hot Wheels models include five top F1 team models, the Cadillac LMP and XMP models, and Terry Cook's Scrape, the radically lowered, ground-hugging maroon Lincoln Zephyr. There is also a '32 Ford Roadster, a 1959 Panel Delivery, a new PT Cruiser, and another concept called Slightly Modified, a track roadster with five inline V-twin motorcycle engines and wildly proportioned trumpet exhausts.

NASCAR rules the 1/24th-scale collectibles, and Mattel obliges the enthusiasts with models of cars from more than twenty of the top teams, along with other collectibles. Michael Kollins, now manager of design for Hot Wheels Collector and Racing, supervises both large-scale operations.

Mattel created the Hot Wheels Hall of Fame exhibit, in conjunction with the Petersen Automotive Museum in Los Angeles. This exhibit celebrates 35 years of Hot Wheels—the people, moments and vehicles that have made automotive and Hot Wheels history. In April 2003, the Petersen Museum unveiled its display of Hot Wheels-inspired full-size cars. From toys that imitate real cars, to real cars inspired by toys, we've come full circle.

"We are delighted to have opened the first permanent Hot Wheels exhibit at the Petersen Automotive Museum to commemorate the 35th Anniversary," said Matt Bousquette, President, Mattel Brands. "And, equally as important is the introduction of the Hot Wheels Hall of Fame that symbolizes the speed, power, performance and attitude that is Hot Wheels."

In November 2003, Mattel in conjunction with the Petersen Automotive Museum, will celebrate the first inductees into the Hot Wheels Hall of Fame. Who will be honored? True to Hot Wheels form, half the fun is in the suspense of waiting to see what Mattel unveils.

Hot Wheels cars turned thirty-five in 2003. That's still at least five years away from middle age, but the accumulation of that much experience, accomplishment, and wisdom undeniably represents the achievement of maturity. An element of that maturity is the fact that car owners will soon be able to put Hot Wheels-brand tires and wheels on their real automobiles. Further evidence is the acquisition of former rival Matchbox on November 18, 1996, and the revitalization of that product line.

"A kid's connection with Hot Wheels starts with his very first car, and it lasts a lifetime," explained Matt Bousquette. "Since 1968 more than 41 million adults have grown up 'driving' Hot Wheels, and more than 800 models and 11,000 variations of Hot Wheels cars have been created. In fact, more than 3 billion Hot Wheels cars have been produced—more than Detroit's 'Big Three' combined since the start of auto manufacturing! Today, Hot Wheels has evolved beyond toys into a lifestyle brand that touches the hearts and minds of guys of all ages spanning many generations because of their connection to their very first car. I'm excited to see what the next 35 years has in store."

Mattel, Inc., was born and has grown up during the twentieth century's baby boom, an era of unparalleled growth in population and personal income. Throughout this time, parents and children used toys to teach each other the magic of potential and the necessity of imagination. Now in the beginning of the twenty-first century, Hot Wheels cars and other toys still allow children to experiment safely and creatively with their futures. With its ever-widening range of cars, trucks, motorcycles, and other vehicles, and its new products under the large umbrella of Hot Wheels Lifestyle, Mattel designers, marketers, and engineers offer a broad view of the future that narrows the gap between young and old.

Beatnik Bandit
Introduced 1968

This classic is one of the original 16 models and continues to roll even today.

Custom Volkswagen
Introduced 1968

This original Redline model is one of the most sought-after VWs. Very rare models came without a sunroof.

Custom Camaro
Introduced 1968

One of the original 16, this model was reportedly the first Hot Wheels car off the line in 1968.

Deora®
Introduced 1968

One of the original 16 cars, the full-sized Deora is now located at the Petersen Automotive Museum in Los Angeles. This is the Sky Show version of the Deora.

Custom Corvette
Introduced 1968

This model, arguably the most popular Hot Wheels car ever, was in stores before the real versions were in dealerships.

Silhouette™
Introduced 1968

This classic original Hot Wheels car has been popular since its introduction and gained new popularity after being remade in 1993.

Custom Fleetside
Introduced 1968

This hugely popular original Redline model was the first Hot Wheels car designed by Harry Bradley, at the request of Elliot Handler. This is the Sky Show version of the Custom Fleetside.

Classic '32 Ford Vicky
Introduced 1969

This classic was remade in 1994 and has since been one of the most popular cars in the lineup.

Custom Mustang
Introduced 1968

This Mustang came with two different hood and window styles. It continues to be popular after it was remade in 1994.

Classic '36 Ford Coupe
Introduced 1969

The model of this car with the rumble seat was later called the Neet Streeter, which had a variety of rare India-only versions.

Splittin' Image®
Introduced 1969

An original classic, this one inspired a new generation when it was remade in 1993.

Heavy Chevy
Introduced 1970

The Camaro from the Spoilers series was remade in 1998 and put in Spectraflame paint in 2002

Twin Mill®
Introduced 1969

This car defines the Hot Wheels name, and a full-sized car was made in 2002.

Heavyweights Ambulance
Introduced 1970

One of the most popular series of the Redline era, the Heavyweights featured 3 cab styles with 4 trailers each.

Volkswagen Beach Bomb
Introduced 1969

Arguably the most popular Hot Wheels ever, the rear-loading version in pink is insured for $100,000.

King 'Kuda
Introduced 1970

This was another of the four Spoilers cars that were redone for the 30th anniversary in 1998.

Boss Hoss
Introduced 1970

Many remember this car in chrome that was included in their Club kit. It's the most popular Mustang in the line.

Light My Firebird
Introduced 1970

This Firebird is as popular now in recent releases as it was when it was first released in 1970.

Classic Nomad
Introduced 1970

This car has been in the line consistently longer than any other, running for almost 34 years.

Mighty Maverick
Introduced 1970

The Maverick had more variations than any other Redline era car. It was later renamed the Street Snorter.

Mongoose
Introduced 1970

A significant part of Hot Wheels history was the racing between the Mongoose and the Snake. Both cars continue to be as popular as ever.

Snake
Introduced 1970

The popular Snake is now immortalized with a full-sized replica at the Petersen Automotive Museum.

Nitty Gritty Kitty™
Introduced 1970

Another model in the Spoilers series, this one was redone in Spectraflame paint over 30 years after it was originally released.

The Demon
Introduced 1970

Based on a real show car, The Demon has reflected the stylings of every era, from Spectraflame to Treasure Hunt.

Paddy Wagon
Introduced 1970

This has been the most popular police car in the lineup and gained new popularity when it was remade in 1993.

Bye-Focal
Introduced 1971

This 1971 Larry Wood classic featured a clear opening hood. It was remade in 2003.

Red Baron
Introduced 1970

A pop culture icon, the Red Baron has gone from Spectraflame paint to fusion graphics over its 33 years.

Classic Cord
Introduced 1971

One of the toughest Redline models to find in any condition, this Larry Wood design is a classic.

Sand Crab
Introduced 1970

This dune buggy is best remembered for the flower stickers it came with. It was later renamed the Dune Daddy.

Evil Weevil®
Introduced 1971

This customized VW in the Spoilers series is very popular and came with racing stickers.

Olds 442
Introduced 1971

One of the top castings of the Redline era and tough to find in any condition, it was later turned into both police cars and taxis.

Motocross 1
Introduced 1975

This was the first Hot Wheels motorcycle.

S'Cool Bus®
Introduced 1971

This Tom Daniel Funny Car is one of the most famous Hot Wheels cars, but has still never been made in Spectraflame paint.

P-911
Introduced 1975

This classic Porsche was in the line for over 25 years before it was retired in 2001.

Side Kick®
Introduced 1972

This model was one of the few cars released in 1972. It had a side that kicked out. It was remade in 1998, but had to have a plastic chassis.

Super Van
Introduced 1975

This is the original billboard vehicle.

Sweet 16
Introduced 1973

One of the three new cars in 1973, this one was remade in 1998, and sparked the Sweet 16 II released later that year.

Corvette Stingray
Introduced 1976

One of the most popular cars in the lineup, this one was featured as part of the Billionth Car series in 1991.

Rodger Dodger
Introduced 1974

This Hot Wheels classic has a blown engine and has been hugely popular since being remade in 1998.

Poison Pinto
Introduced 1976

This souped-up Pinto had some rare versions and is now being remade with metal chassis and engine.

'31 Doozie
Introduced 1977

This has been one of the classics since its 1977 release. It was retired in 2003.

'57 T-Bird
Introduced 1978

This is probably second only to the '57 Chevy in number of versions, and has recently had the porthole version return to the line.

'57 Chevy
Introduced 1977

This casting has been used more than any other. Many collectors collect only this car.

Hot Bird®
Introduced 1978

This one is a pure classic. However, it seemed to disappear after 1997.

GMC Motor Home
Introduced 1977

This motor home has had many India-only versions since its release. It has been released recently as a Jones Soda promo.

Auburn 852
Introduced 1979

This one never lasted long on the shelves and is as popular as ever.

Letter Getter
Introduced 1977

First issued as a mail truck, it has been released many times since.

Bywayman
Introduced 1979

Many generations of kids have grown up with this standard Hot Wheels truck that was retired after nearly 25 years of service.

Second Wind®
Introduced 1977

This one has appeared sparingly throughout the years, and last appeared in 1997.

Split Window '63
Introduced 1980

Probably the most popular Corvette in the lineup today, this one was initially a Hi-Raker and has had many different names in its 20-plus years.

'40s Woodie
Introduced 1980

This one, originally a Hi-Raker, has been a Cal Custom with surfboards and is a premiums' favorite.

'55 Chevy
Introduced 1982

This one, while not as popular as the '57 Chevy, has been very popular despite the fact it doesn't have an interior. It was retired in 2001.

3-Window '34
Introduced 1980

This one, originally released as a Hi-Raker, has been everything from a Treasure Hunt to a Malt-O-Meal premium.

Camaro Z-28
Introduced 1982

The Camaro seems to have sported more wacky '80s tampo designs than any other car.

Hiway Hauler®
Introduced 1980

One of the most popular castings that feature great logos and artwork, this one was remade in 1992 and has been equally as popular.

Mercedes 380 SEL
Introduced 1982

This was the most popular Mercedes casting and retired in 1999. This was a favorite because of the dog in the window.

Old Number 5®
Introduced 1981

This Larry Wood design is the most popular fire truck in the line and shows up sparingly for premium releases.

'40s Ford 2-Door
Introduced 1983

This heavy Ford has been a collector favorite since its initial release.

'35 Classic Cadillac
Introduced 1982

The Classic Caddy was one of the original 1995 Treasure Hunt models and has been featured in a variety of great designs over the years.

'67 Camaro
Introduced 1983

A modernized version of the original Camaro, this one with an opening hood is arguably the most popular car in the basic line today.

Classic Cobra
Introduced 1983

This classic car features an opening hood and has sported many premium decorations since its inception.

Good Humor Truck
Introduced 1984

This model has been everything from a BBQ stop, food van, skate rental and, of course, ice cream truck.

Classic Packard
Introduced 1983

The Packard has only ever been released in black and after disappearing in 1983, it reappeared in 1997 in China, where it disappeared again.

Ferrari Testarossa
Introduced 1987

This sports car, which moved the Hot Wheels brand into the '90s, was modernized in 1998 into the F512M.

Double Deck Bus
Introduced 1983

This model has had many rare, India-only versions.

Talbot Lago
Introduced 1988

This exotic car always seems to be tough to find, though no tougher than the #714 version released in 1997.

'65 Mustang
Introduced 1984

Another popular Mustang, this one with a metal base and opening hood is one of the more popular cars in the line.

'32 Ford Delivery
Introduced 1989

This classic Ford has had many rare premium editions, including the Temecula Rod Run.

Baja Bug
Introduced 1984

The Baja Bug with exposed exhaust often features knobby Real Riders tires.

T-Bucket
Introduced 1989

This Ford Model T has a full-sized version that was replicated into 1/64th scale in 2002. It has not been in the basic line since 1995.

VW Bug
Introduced 1989

The most widely produced car ever, the Hot Wheels versions are always extremely popular.

'58 Corvette
Introduced 1995

The first new model of 1995, this one featured a blown motor in early releases.

Purple Passion®
Introduced 1990

This car caused as much frenzy in 1990 as the VW Bus did in 1996. It has been released as a special edition countless times.

1970 Dodge Charger Daytona
Introduced 1996

This popular model was first released with a metal base.

Limozeen
Introduced 1991

Moms, dads, kids and collectors alike all love the limo, which is why it doesn't last long on the shelves. The most popular version is the all-gold 1995 version.

VW Bus
Introduced 1996

The most popular casting of recent history, this car is also the heaviest in the line.

'56 Flashsider
Introduced 1992

One of the most popular trucks in the lineup, this '56 Chevy has never had an interior.

'33 Ford Convertible
Introduced 1997

This was originally released in the *Home Improvement* Action Pack and has been popular ever since.

'93 Camaro
Introduced 1993

Originally in the Demolition Man series, this model has had many race team style decos.

'59 Chevy Impala
Introduced 1997

Many tough versions of this one have shown up in playsets. This was retooled in 2003 into a 1959 Bel Air.

'67 GTO
Introduced 1997

A pleasant surprise, this model showed up unexpectedly in a 1997 limited set.

Dairy Delivery™
Introduced 1998

With one of the largest deco spaces of any car, this is one of the heaviest cars when using a metal chassis.

'70 Plymouth Barracuda
Introduced 1997

One of the few cars to have two window tools that allow it to be either a hardtop or convertible.

Go Kart
Introduced 1998

This small model has big popularity, and every version has gone quickly soon after its release.

Scorchin' Scooter®
Introduced 1997

The toughest vehicle of 1997, this was the first motorcycle released in nearly 20 years.

Mustang Mach I
Introduced 1998

This one gained notoriety when the color was quickly changed from orange to yellow in its first year.

'32 Ford
Introduced 1998

This classic roadster has become a favorite for use in limited editions.

Tail Dragger®
Introduced 1998

This classic hot rod features a metal chassis and always looks good with pinstripes or flames.

'70 Roadrunner
Introduced 1998

This is another muscle car that has become a favorite for premiums.

'56 Ford
Introduced 1999

Collectors love this model because of its opening hood. It was one of the toughest cars of 1999.

1970 Chevelle SS
Introduced 1999

This classic muscle car has never looked better than in Spectraflame red when released in 2002.

'71 Plymouth GTX
Introduced 2001

This popular muscle car never looked better than in Spectraflame antifreeze green in its 2003 release.

Ford GT-40
Introduced 1999

One of the most classic roadsters, the first versions of this one had a narrow rear wheel that was later changed.

Evil Twin
Introduced 2001

A modern Larry Wood classic, this model features two large blown engines.

Anglia Panel Truck
Introduced 2000

This popular panel also featured an opening hood and has been used in many premium editions.

'40 Ford Coupe
Introduced 2002

Arguably the most popular car of 2002, this has been done as a premium more times than any other car since 2002.

Mini Cooper
Introduced 2000

With its pop-open body this Mini was popular even before the craze.

'68 Cougar
Introduced 2002

This model became popular when a rare transition version appeared from a premium run.

Shoe Box
Introduced 2000

This classic has been released as a taxi and was also the first car to feature PR5 wheels.

Vairy 8
Introduced 2003

This customized Corvair has a metal chassis and was one of the first cars to have small five-spoke front wheels.

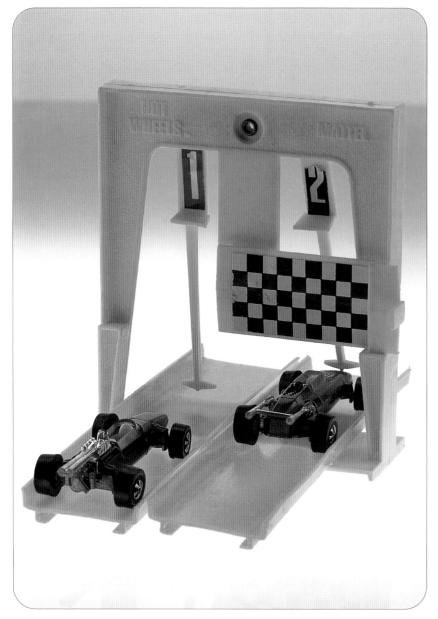